The Ultimate Guide to

North Minneapolis Real Estate

What you need to know BEFORE

Buying and Selling a Home

On the North Side

Copyright 2014 Vork Real Estate Group LLC

www.constancevork.com

I	How to Use This Book	4
II	Welcome to North Minneapolis	7

SECTION ONE – FOR SELLERS

Chapter One: How to Have Great Showings and Get Top Dollar for Your Home — 12

Chapter Two: You Only Get One Chance to Make a First Impression — 23

Chapter Three: Read This Before You Hire a Listing Agent — 38

Chapter Four: What You Need To Know Before Listing Your Home — 54

Chapter Five: Does Your Agent Know How to Sell Luxury Homes? — 88

Chapter Six: Should You Sell Your Home without an Agent? Insider Tips for Marketing Your Home for Sale by Owner — 108

SECTION TWO – FOR BUYERS

Chapter Seven: Choosing the Real Estate Agent that is Right for *You* — 112

Chapter Eight: The Fifteen Most Costly Mistakes Made by Homebuyers and How to Avoid Them — 132

Chapter Nine: Are you a First-Time Homebuyer? Six Things You MUST Do — 205

Chapter Ten: Investing in Rental Property on the Northside — 219

SECTION THREE – FOR SELLERS AND BUYERS

Chapter Eleven: *WHO IS THE CLOSER AND WHAT IS THIS ABOUT TITLE INSURANCE? –By Lynn Gleason Oberpriller* — 230

Chapter Twelve *THE MORTGAGE CHAPTER –By Paul Basil, Megastar Financial* — 236

Chapter Thirteen: How Staging Will Get You a Higher Price for Your Home — 242

Conclusion — 247

Acknowledgments — 251

I

HOW TO USE THIS BOOK

This book is fundamentally a basics of buying and selling real estate. The vast majority of concepts included here are widely applicable, regardless of the community in which you own or are shopping. The chapters are divided into three sections, the first addressing would-be sellers, the second addressing buyers, and the third addressing information that affects both sides.

Of course I think everyone should read the entire thing, and not just because it's my book. Buying and selling real estate typically involves negotiation. Sometimes large amounts of money can be shaved off of a listing price. Sometimes a listing number represents a starting point from which buyers take price soaring through multiple offers.

Given this, it seems reasonable that a person wishing to maximize their total gain (whether on the buying side or the selling side) might be well-advised to consider the psychology of the other end of the transaction. Reading the chapters dedicated to those other sides can help give you perspective as you prepare to embark upon your purchase or sale. At least that is my hope.

Where this book differs from others, obviously, is that it written with North Minneapolis in mind. And it is not just for investors who wish to swoop in from out of town and scoop all of our low-priced real estate.

We are finally emerging from what has been one of the worst (if not THE worst) times for the North Minneapolis real estate market. When I first began working in this community, there were precious few agents who would even consider the area. I heard story after story of buyers who asked about Northside addresses, only to be talked out of visiting those homes by their agents. Likewise, I heard a number of sellers describe agents who didn't return calls, or who –if they did show up to discuss listing- were clearly not interested in giving their best efforts.

Things have changed though, and are continuing to change. More and more people are recognizing North Minneapolis for its unique and varied neighborhoods, excellent parks, proximity to Downtown, and relatively affordable housing stock.

Things are on the up-swing. I'm excited to be a part of that. And glad for my fellow Northsiders, who deserve it.

II

WELCOME TO NORTH MINNEAPOLIS

I attended a conference recently at the Minneapolis Convention Center. Arranged and hosted by the City of Minneapolis, and designed for residents and members of our many neighborhood organizations, the theme was *Common Ground: A City that Works for All.*

While there, I noticed a curious thing. It seemed to me that an inordinate number of the participants, workshops, and conversations were rooted in our city's Northside. Indeed, the underlying theme seemed as though it might have been described as *Minneapolis: A City that Has Finally Decided to Address its Weakest Link.*

It's no secret to anyone who has lived in our state that Minneapolis's Northside has a long-established reputation. And while much of that has been overblown (I promise you that you will not get shot if you come to my house) there are some truths that go along with being the least affluent, least developed, and dare I say least understood part of our major metropolitan area.

We have uglier commercial thoroughfares than the rest of town. We have more trash in our streets. We have more murders assigned to our Northside addresses. When the housing market took its great nose-dive of the preceding decade, we played host to a whopping fifty percent of our entire city's foreclosures. We are vying with the most affluent part of town for the most demolitions, though while theirs are to build mega-houses, ours are to correct blight, and the vacant lots that remain are perhaps even more depressing than the empty, frozen-up houses which preceded them.

But those stories have already been told.

What I hope to weave through this guide to North Minneapolis real estate are some of the _other_ stories. The stories you may have begun to hear little snippets of, since you have decided to read this book. The stories that Northside residents mostly know, but that newcomers need to be told, sometimes more than once before they'll get curious enough to come check things out.

The other stories – better stories- about this Northside; this land of 58,000 residents, making their homes and raising their families in thirteen (or fifteen, depending on who you ask) distinct neighborhoods.

I want you to know the stories about the community gardens that bring neighbors together in Willard-Hay. And about the wine and cheese parties in the opulent Victorians of Old Highland. And the outdoor movies and music of *Live on the Drive*, where residents of both Minneapolis and Robbinsdale mingle along the grand median of Victory Memorial Drive.

There are people who will tell you about how North Minneapolis used to be great, back in the 40s or 50s. Back before the race riots on Plymouth Avenue, before the Jewish residents mostly all departed for places like St. Louis Park and Golden Valley. And there are people who will tell you how great North Minneapolis is going to be, as homebuyers and renters alike return to the city, beaten down by gasoline prices and the foreclosure hangover of so many exurban McMansion developments.

But I am here to tell you what you and only a few others probably already know... and that is that North Minneapolis is also great right now. And that is why so many of us live here. It's also why the interest I've received from potential homebuyers here has skyrocketed.

We have some of the most affordable high-quality housing in the city of Minneapolis. Many of our neighborhoods are just minutes to downtown. Other parts are exceptionally convenient to various corporate employers along the western corridors of Highways 100, 55 and 394. And while we don't have the chain of lakes like our friends to the southwest, we can lay claim to the 759 acres of year-round beauty that is our city's single greatest park: Theodore Wirth Park.

We have so much to offer, in fact, that I might be reduced to using a cliché here… that North Minneapolis could be called our City's _best kept secret._

SECTION ONE

FOR SELLERS

CHAPTER ONE

HOW TO HAVE GREAT SHOWINGS AND GET TOP DOLLAR FOR YOUR HOME

What I'm about to tell you is uncomfortable for some people to hear.

I don't really know why, but for some reason, it's just really hard for some people. Even though it's common knowledge, and frankly *common sense*, many people selling their homes completely ignore this.

It's almost mind boggling as a real estate agent to see this over and over and over again. Well, *frustrating* is probably the right word.

Sellers who ignore the advice in this chapter consistently get less for their home than they otherwise would, and SHOULD, get. In fact, one of these easiest ways to ensure your home sells for less money--**or doesn't sell at all**--is to ignore this chapter. So, please don't ignore it.

Here we go:

I know you love having the art work your children or grandchildren created displayed prominently all over your refrigerator, but to be honest, the buyers really don't.

And when it comes to selling ANYTHING (not just real estate) **it is the buyer that matters**.

Not the seller.

If you are selling your home, you need to completely DE-CLUTTER and DEPERSONALIZE it. All of the things that make your house a "home" are precisely those which need to go. I know this is blunt advice, maybe even a little rude, but it must be said. I know many real estate agents out there are *thinking* it, but some are too timid to tell their clients the truth.

If you don't depersonalize and de-clutter your home, you will get less money for it than you should.

If it sells at all.

Let's get into specifics.

The refrigerator is just *one* area that we see decorated that shouldn't be.

As long as we are discussing the kitchen, if you have any small appliances sitting out, put them in a cupboard. I know you use your toaster daily, as well as some other items, but if whatever it is doesn't look good in a photo, put it away.

And that goes for the rest of the "stuff" in your house that buyers don't want to see. Think of your home as one of those model homes sold by a housing developer. They are bare—the idea is to create the psychological impression on potential buyers that this could be **their** home. That this IS their home.

It almost goes without saying that creating this impression is really difficult if your personal items are everywhere.

Here's a quick list of things to hide or put away:

- Toaster, mixer, and other kitchen appliances
- Family photos
- Knick knacks
- Book collections
- Posters

- Paintings
- Dirty diapers
- Anything on your fridge (photos, magnets, etcetera)
- Magazines on the coffee table
- Newspapers
- Awards or certifications on the wall/shelves

As you can probably tell by reading this list, your house needs to be BARE. Completely depersonalized. I'm not kidding—this can be worth thousands of dollars to you in the final sale price.

Real estate is just as much art as it is science. Part of the art side of selling a home is value *perception*. And the perceived value of your home is much higher when it's clean, de-cluttered, and depersonalized.

Let me tell you about one house that I went into **where I actually scolded the owner**--*and it wasn't even my listing*.

I was showing a property to some first time home buyers. They were really excited to see a certain house because it was very close to their best friend's place. We walked in the door and **the first thing we saw was a sink full of dirty dishes.**

Not just kind of dirty. Dishes that had MOLDY food on them.

This is not an exaggeration.

There was literally MOLD on the food. It was absolutely disgusting. Like, the kind of disgusting that makes you want to throw up. But, well, in the interest of keeping calm in case my clients were able to see past that, I tried my hardest to not puke.

The counter top had every appliance known to mankind on it, and every item was filthy. If I had known the condition of this place before scheduling the showing, I would have contacted the nearest nuclear power plant and ordered some HazMat suits for my clients. You know, full body rubber suits, gas masks and the whole nine yards. And that's assuming I was willing to risk their lives to show the property. Only God knows the amount of carcinogens and bacteria that was **on display** in this home.

I wouldn't wish it on my worst enemies.

It's not like there was some mold in the walls of the basement. That's still a problem, but at least it's a bit more common and understandable. But ON YOUR DIRTY DISHES IN THE SINK? Seriously?

Going into the living room I had to yell out, "Watch your step!"

This was to protect their shoes from animal feces.

BUT WAIT-----there's more:

The centerpiece on the coffee table was a soiled diaper. Yep, you read that right. A diaper full of poop.

Now, I'll be honest--real estate agents are notorious for finding creative euphemisms to describe undesirable characteristics of homes. You know, words and phrases like "fixer upper potential," "cute and cozy," or my personal favorite, "needs some TLC."

Folks, when you see a home that **needs some TLC** (tender, loving care) this means that the interior is probably so outdated that the orange carpet in the family room is 10 years newer than everything else.

Anyway...

At this point in the story you probably think I'm exaggerating to prove a point.

I promise you that I am not.

Like I said, real estate agents have a lot of clever words and phrases used to rationalize undesirable features. To my knowledge, a euphemism has yet to be coined which addresses the problem of diapers of poop on the coffee table. Here's my suggestion for future agents who encounter this common problem: refer to it as "homemaker friendly." Apparently changing the baby's diaper on the coffee table is super-convenient. Who knew?

I have NO idea how anyone cleaned up—or bathed—because the tub was filled with empty soup cans and garbage. Yes. You read that correctly. The bathtub was literally filled with garbage.

Now, I'm not that creative of a person. I'm really not. I couldn't make this story up. It's stranger than fiction.

The McDonald's wrappers and half eaten cheeseburger on the bed in the master bedroom was also a nice touch.

That's where I unleashed.

Those of you reading this who know me might be aware of

the fact that I need to work on my profanity a little bit, especially now that I have a young child. But I do generally keep my language PG while in professional settings. However, I lost control of my tongue for a second when I saw that cheeseburger. Something along the lines of "Oh you have GOT TO BE @%@%$ KIDDING ME."

Needless to say, the buyers did not purchase that house. And for some odd reason, I don't believe anyone else did either. Weird, huh?

Anyway, that's an extreme example of what not to do, clearly. Let's get back to less extreme (but still very important) aspects to de-personalization and de-cluttering.

Family photos can sometimes be a touchy subject.

Most agents will tell you that it's okay to have a couple family photos out, but if your entire house looks like a shrine, you need to tone it down. Personally, I recommend ZERO family photos. The reason is that even if you just have a couple, tastefully placed around among your staging items, it still comes across as *your* house to the prospective buyers. And however lovely it may be, buyers want to find *their* house.

It's really difficult for buyers to picture themselves in a home when at every turn, they are seeing framed photos of all six children from birth through graduation, plus the dog in various poses on your couch or catching a Frisbee in mid-air. (Somebody please tell my husband this if we ever decide to sell our place in Homewood.) Really, I have actually seen this.

Oh, and collectibles. Knick knacks. Can't forget those!

I once ran across a "Gnome" collector. This person had every shelf and every cupboard full of gnomes. Honestly, this person had lined up every open space of each and every wall throughout the entire house with gnomes.

Every size and color ever created. It was actually a bit frightening.

Now, I have nothing against gnomes. I understand that they've become rather popular for traveling the world with, in fact. (I once saw a guy walk into a café on a small island off the coast of Honduras carrying a gnome the size of a toddler.) But when it comes to presenting a house for sale, I don't care if it's gnomes, Precious Moments, model planes, autographed baseballs, poopy diapers, or wine bottles. PACK THEM UP.

Oh, and speaking of packing up... <u>Your garage should not serve as a repository of non-vehicle-related things.</u>

If you haven't used something in a year, *get rid of it.*

Here's a classic story: I am touring a house and am pleasantly surprised at how hard the sellers have worked to get it ready to place on the market.

Then we go into the garage.

No wonder their cars are in the driveway. Is the floor dirt, or concrete, or what? I don't know because I can't see it!

That's when I hear this, "Well, when we bought new furniture 10 years ago, we saved this so when our son goes to college...."

Their son was two years old.

Another good one is, "Well, Uncle Frank passed away a few years back and we inherited his stuff. We just haven't had time to go through it yet."

GIVE. IT. UP.

Chances are that your kids won't like it or want it. Give it to someone who can actually use it. There are a lot of organizations out there that would be happy to take it. Let them!

Clutter doesn't just apply to the house. *It also applies to outdoor spaces.* We'll get to that in the next chapter.

CHAPTER TWO

YOU ONLY GET ONE CHANCE TO MAKE A FIRST IMPRESSION

You've probably heard the expression *curb appeal* before. It's not some secret marketing strategy used by Realtors. Everybody knows about curb appeal. But not everyone realizes precisely *how* important it actually is.

Advertising gurus say that the headline is the most important part of the ad. Why? Because if the headline doesn't grab your attention, you won't read the rest! You have to get people to read the headline first. Real estate is no different.

Your curb appeal is your "headline."

You are selling not just your house, but the land it sits on also. If you think cleaning out your garage means "place it alongside the house," you couldn't be more wrong.

Pulling up to a house that has either a car collection in the driveway, old couches or other old furniture stacked up behind it, and/or poopy diapers on the front lawn greatly takes away from the curb appeal. Trust me on this one.

One more story:

This one is my personal favorite. I'm showing a house in late May, but the bright orange pumpkin lawn and leaf bags still adorn the house as if those bags are an artful piece of landscaping.

Seriously folks, Halloween was seven months prior! Are you that lazy where you're not willing to spend ten minutes cleaning up the yard to boost the curb appeal? This could mean thousands of dollars in the final sales price, because it directly affects the *emotionally-driven* **perceived value.**

Remember, most people start their home search on the Internet. If your house is not appealing *outside*, chances are they won't go *inside*. It's like going fishing without bait. Do that and you probably won't catch anything.

Another thing to remember on the outside is the *not-so-pleasant* subject of pet waste. Some surprises are good, but when you step in a steamy pile of doggy doo on a hot summer day, it's not so good. That person will probably not buy your house.

Seriously people, we do not live in a war-zone. If a buyer has to dodge the bombs as if walking through a live minefield, it might be time to clean up the yard.

When it comes to cleaning and/or organizing, **put it on the top of your priority list.** If you don't have time, get up earlier in the morning. It's really that important.

If you can't do that, try hiring it out, or bribing a friend. I have found that if I ask a friend, not only can it be enjoyable for us both, but we can exchange time where I help them with a project at their house later on. It's a win-win.

Let me ask you this: **if you are in the market for a new car**, how impressed would you be if there were empty fast food bags, containers of half eaten fries, gum wrappers, and some dirty laundry inside? Or to go with perhaps a more reasonable example, what if it was just all dusty inside? Or smelled faintly of cigarettes? Car dealers would NEVER put a car on the for sale lot until it was completely clean and detailed. They often pay professional cleaners to make sure it's spotless!

It is standard in the car industry to make sure the product is clean. And, well, it's standard in **pretty much every other industry too.** When was the last time you went to the mall and there was garbage in a retail store? Or a dirty, smelly restaurant? It would be an outrage. And I'm guessing you would not return.

When we buy a thing, we expect it to be clean. It's not a nice extra, or a bonus. It's the price of entry. It's *expected.*

Here's what I'm getting at: People are SHOPPING when they tour your home. If retail stores maintain an immaculate level of cleanliness to sell thirty-dollar shirts, shouldn't you present your home with an equal attention to detail? After all, most homes are a few hundred thousand dollars or more!

When you stop and think about it, it's crazy that anyone would buy a home that wasn't absolutely spotless. I would go as far as to recommend hiring professional cleaners if you *really* want your home to sell quickly. It *does* make a difference in how well your home shows.

And while we're on the topic of cleaning, can I talk about another matter?

Odor.

It may be surprising if you haven't bought a house recently, or ever, but buyers often put a name on each house they see, in order to help them remember which is which. And those names often have to do with the smells.

I remember selling the hampster house, the cat house, the candle house, the cookie house, and most recently, *the vomit house*. (That last one actually rivaled the poopy diaper house.)

From the outside, the vomit house was a storybook cottage. It looked like the Hansel and Gretel house. Just beautiful! I almost expected gingerbread cookies to be baking when we walked in.

Unfortunately, when I opened the door, the buyers' reaction was to run back to the car!

The house had been vacant for over a month and the garbage was not taken out. Not only that, but someone had left the freezer full of meat, and the power had gone out.

Yes, that's right.

There are no words to describe those smells. Let me just say that taking my clients out to lunch after was probably the cheapest tab I have ever paid.

When it comes to human memory, guess which of the five senses is strongest? Yep---smell!

Scientists have documented that smells send powerful signals to the memory center of our brain, the hypothalamus. In fact, the olfactory system is part of the brain's *limbic system*. The limbic system is responsible for memories and emotions.

When you smell a new scent for the first time, your brain wants to link it to something - an event, a person, a thing, or even a moment. Your brain forges a connection between the smell and a memory -- associating the smell of **chlorine** with summers at the pool or the aroma of hotdogs and popcorn with a baseball game.

When you encounter the smell again, *the link is already there*, ready to evoke a memory or a mood.

What does this mean for you as a home-seller? It means that people will REMEMBER what your house smells like. Because of its location in the brain's limbic system, the buyers' smell sense will inform their memory of your home, and link it to a feeling about your property.

If you're trying to sell your home for top dollar, even the slightest unpleasant odors can ruin a potential sale.

Unpleasant smells can detract from an otherwise lovely home!

That being said, your home can smell great, but if it hasn't been updated since the Carter administration, well, don't expect to get top dollar.

Or any dollar.

So there's what NOT to do.

But here's something you've probably heard before that you *should* do. And if you haven't already, what are you waiting for?

Here it is:

PAINT.

Let me say that again, and maybe again after that.

PAINT. PAINT. PAINTPAINTPAINT.

Fresh, neutral paint is <u>the most inexpensive way to boost the value of your home</u>. Period. Hands-down.

You may think little Johnny's finger-painting is cute on his bedroom wall (next to all the photos of him and Shadow the dog?) but the buyers will beg to differ.

Over time, if you have changed your artwork around, moved furniture around, your home may have accumulated some scratches or other "wall injuries."

The sponge paint house...yup, a house that will forever be dubbed that. I don't just mean the interior. I mean the exterior. All of it.

Let me give you a rule of thumb:

If you drive around your city, look on the internet, or get ideas from *Pinterest*, **and don't see anything remotely close to what you're thinking of for a paint scheme**, don't do it.

Different is fine *if you are staying in your home.*

If you're selling, however, that is not the time to be daring. If you have old awnings, remove them. Old faded shutters - either paint them, or remove them. Sometimes it's as simple as getting out the pressure washer.

Spiders, dirt, and general uncleanliness can make your house look neglected. Remember: your home should be SPOTLESS before selling. Not clean in a general sense, but *spotless*. As in, able to pass a white glove test.

I'll again return to the car metaphor: your home should be as clean as a brand new car. Even if it was built in the 1940's, it should still *feel* like a new home.

Your home is a PRODUCT and you are displaying it!

You've probably heard people say "It's the little things." And that is true. We haven't been covering big-ticket items here so far – no renovations or upgrades, but simply maintenance items. It all matters.

I know, I know... Sometimes it can be hard to objectively look at your home from the perspective of a buyer, but that is exactly what you need to do. Sellers who miss this step may have listings sit on the market for months and months, sometimes even having a birthday.

Note: your home should not have a "for sale" birthday. If it's been on the market for an entire year, something is wrong.

In general, a home should not take more than ninety days to sell. If it hasn't had multiple showings, inquiries, and offers before ninety days, something is wrong. (Often this means it's overpriced, but there can be a variety of factors at play).

Again, this is *general* advice. In some markets and neighborhoods, demand is simply lower, and a house might sit for one hundred and sixty days. It all depends on supply and demand, and how long you are comfortable waiting. Or how long you can *afford* to wait for your home to sell.

What many sellers don't realize is the more days on the market a home racks up, the more its reputation suffers. Most buyers will become suspicious if a home has been on the market for a long time. They'll subconsciously think something is wrong with it, or that it's extremely overpriced (even if it is only *slightly* overpriced). Don't let this happen to you.

This is where you need a brutally honest agent (or a trusted friend) to walk through your home as if they were purchasing it.

When they pull into the driveway, does it look inviting? Is the grass arm-pit high? Is your trash bin overflowing in the driveway? Are there flower pots full of dead flowers--or worse yet--sun faded, plastic flowers? Upon walking in the door, do you smell a nice scented candle? Or do you smell a cat box?

Oh, and speaking of bad smells, make sure your toilet is flushed. Yeah, I know what you're thinking: *Thanks, Captain Obvious. Duh!*

Well, I'm sure you're not the person who'd be so silly as to overlook such a thing. But you'd be surprised how many others do just that.

I have shown properties where bathrooms have not been checked.

This is NOT a good surprise to leave for potential buyers.

And as long as we're talking about leaving things behind for potential buyers, let's also address your *valuables*. PLEASE, for your sake and the sake of the showing agent, put them away.

I actually had this happen to me, and I'm not making this

up: I was showing my own house. The parents kept me busy in the living room while their teenage daughter went to use the restroom. (That is NOT where she went.) I thought it took a little too long and they left in a hurry. I quickly ran into my bedroom and noticed *my diamond necklace from Greece was missing.*

I quickly ran out after them and confronted the issue. Luckily, they (very reluctantly) cooperated and I got the necklace back.

Those people never contacted me again and as I learned, they didn't use their real names when they looked at the house. Fortunately, nowadays, agents pre-qualify their buyers and generally get a bank letter so their identity is not so easy to forge.

And that brings me to another important issue: make sure the agent showing your house has actually *qualified* their buyers. There are documented stories about agents who were attacked, or houses that were scoped out during a showing--only for the "buyer" to go back to the property later and help themselves to televisions, jewelry, and more.

I'm not saying this to fear-monger. It is a real, documented problem.

How does that make you feel about selling yourself as a "for sale by owner?"

Again, I'm not trying to scare you. But it is critical to be aware of potential risks when letting strangers into your home.

And speaking of doing things yourself, if you're not qualified... don't do it.

That also holds true for hiring the least expensive contractor for the job. Is he insured? Do they have a list of testimonials from past clients? Are they "legit?"

Here's a story of what happened when I hired the cheapest guy for the job one time:

True to character, I purchased a real fixer-upper, over in the Hawthorne neighborhood. The home had belonged to an elderly man who had occupied it for approximately sixty years, and it didn't appear that he had EVER done any maintenance. The lovely original plaster was badly cracking in many spots and entirely missing in others, where years of water intrusion from a bad roof had dislodged it from the lath.

So among other contractors, I hired a guy to do sheetrock patches in the spots where the plaster had been compromised. (This of course was AFTER the roof had been replaced.)

I should mention that one of the reasons I bought this house was that it had tremendous original character. North Minneapolis has a wealth of older homes with gorgeous features like un-painted woodwork, built-ins, and so forth. This house in particular featured columned room-dividers, intact pocket doors, an open stairway, original fixtures, and a beautiful kitchen pantry with original maple cabinetry, among other things.

So the house was vacant, and I gave the guy a lockbox combination. I was pregnant at the time, and not spending the hours over at this property that I might have in the past. This was a mistake.

There were so many ridiculous things that resulted from this guy's presence in my property that I can't even list them all. But the big one was this: he GUTTED and DESTROYED my original pantry. That's right. When I told him to replace the damaged plaster ceiling and sheetrock it, he apparently heard me say "rip out all that original cabinetry, all the plaster behind it, and leave me with a sheetrock

BOX off the rear of my kitchen." Oh, and then he also decided to paint the trim in a bedroom, even though I had never asked him to paint. Nor did I provide the celery-green color that he decided to use. Very strange indeed...

Don't let this be you. Learn from the mistakes of others and vet your contractors well. In fact, if you need help, ask your Realtor! (And if that turns out to be me, I PROMISE you I will not give you the weird sheetrock guy. I learned my lesson.)

CHAPTER THREE

READ THIS BEFORE YOU HIRE A LISTING AGENT

Let's talk for a minute about real estate agents. Specifically, how to pick the agent that is right for *you*.

There is a sense of mystery out there concerning how the real estate industry works. I'd like to shed some light on that. Before giving you my opinion (and some helpful analysis), let's begin with a list of facts many people don't know about real estate agents and the "business model."

- Real estate agents are usually independent contractors, not employees.
- Most of us work on **straight commission.** We do not receive a salary.
- Most agents do not receive an advertising allowance, a client entertainment allowance, or an allowance of any kind. We pay for everything out of our own pockets.
- Usually the agent's broker takes a cut of the

commission check. It varies from brokerage to brokerage. *Sometimes it is a scale that adjusts based on how many homes an agent has sold throughout the year, and/or how many active listings they have.* For example, the more homes an agent sells or the greater number of listings they procure, the higher percentage of the commission they keep. This means they make more profit (as a percentage of the commission) in the later months of the year. This is true for some, but not all, agents.

- As it is documented in many best-selling personal development books for real estate agents, **the easiest way to get rich selling real estate is to get as many listings as possible** (I'll touch on that topic later in the book). *Sometimes this is at odds with what is best for the client.*
- Many agents also have to pay a "desk fee" (rent for keeping a desk in an office).
- There will be additional closing costs above and beyond paying the agent's commission. These are

always negotiable between the buyer and seller.

- Agents incur a lot more expenses selling (or helping you purchase) a home than most people realize. *Just one example* is the price of gasoline and wear and tear on a vehicle. When you're constantly driving to meetings and showing homes, the miles can add up pretty quickly! Personally, I drive about 30,000 miles a year assuming I don't take any additional road trips or vacations out of state. With the price of gasoline continually climbing, it's a major expense.

- Just as is the case in other professions, **there are different levels of certification and expertise for real estate agents.** For example, did you know that the term "Realtor" isn't merely a general term for a real estate agent? All Realtors are licensed real estate agents, but *not all real estate agents are certified Realtors.* There are a few other certifications, too: ABR, CRS, CRP, GRI, etc.

- According to the *National Association of Realtors* 2013 Member Survey, the median income for Realtors is $33,500. For the most part, real estate agents are not making big bucks. Exceptions prove the rule.

- We all have our listings on each other's web sites. The industry term for this is "Broker Reciprocity."
- Any licensed agent out there can show any company's listings--unless the seller doesn't want it that way (which is rare).
- It will take a few hours for an agent to do the proper research and create what's called a CMA (Comparative Market Analysis). A CMA is a report that tells home sellers what their home is worth, **and at what price it should be listed.** Some agents have software that automatically generates a report by pulling data from the MLS. These automatically generated documents start out rather unreliable (think Zillow) as they have no capacity to account for things like curb appeal, cleanliness, and unusual features that may make a house special. Because of this, it's important that such reports are carefully reviewed and adjusted for a home's specific

circumstances by the agent preparing them.

- Federal fair housing law prohibits real estate agents from talking about certain things in certain ways. The best example of this is neighborhood demographics. Agents are prohibited by law from encouraging buyers to select (or not select) a given neighborhood based on the racial or ethnic makeup of that neighborhood, for example. Neither are we supposed to describe any particular neighborhood as "bad." Most of the agents I know who both live and work in North Minneapolis are acutely sensitive to this, and will properly direct their clients to non-agent resources (such as websites addressing crime statistics and other neighborhood data) rather than categorizing. *Agents hailing from outside of North Minneapolis (and, in particular, outside of the city itself) are much more prone to goofing this one up.* I have heard stories of many of them who in fact will tell clients that they do not wish to show homes on the Northside because they fear for their safety. (This is a crock, and their clients should fire them for it.) The worst though may well be suburban LISTING agents, who somehow manage to procure a Northsider's listing and then treat it like it is diseased. One recent example of this was a magnificent house on Penn Avenue that was listed by a Woodbury agent. When I requested a showing of the property, I was twice informed that there was no lockbox on the (vacant) property, and that the door should be open.

Seriously. *This agent thought so little of the house, neighborhood and NEIGHBORS that she didn't even bother to come down to the property and see that it was secured.* Insulting! (Somewhat tangentially, I found the property locked upon my first attempt to view it. A phone call to the agent left her staff completely befuddled. They had not secured it! It was supposed to be open! Hmm... they were going to have to send out a locksmith. I laughed all the way home, imagining that some irate neighbor had had enough of an unsecured property on their block and gone and put a lock on it themselves. Or perhaps a wily buyer who wanted to make sure no competition had the chance to see the house before he/she could get an offer in.)

In any event, now that you've gotten a summary the business model of real estate, let's dive into picking the agent that's right for you.

What I'm about to say might ruffle a few agents' feathers, but it must be done:

If you want the best service, hire a full time agent.

Consider this: full time agents devote their entire day to buying and selling real estate for their clients. It's not a hobby or a part time gig; it's their career. Full time agents spend *at least* forty hours a week serving their clients. I've found it's typically fifty to sixty hours, even up to seventy hours during peak selling season.

Again, to be brutally honest, there is no way a part time agent who is trying to make some extra spending money will have the expertise and knowledge that a full time agent does. Do you really want to trust the purchase or sale of a $200,000 asset (or a million dollar asset, for that matter) to someone who is *dabbling* in real estate?

Full time agents are immersed daily in the world of real estate. In fact, most full time agents I know don't even need to do much research to create a market analysis for someone wanting to sell their home in that agent's target area—after a quick tour, we can quote a pretty accurate listing price. The reason is that we work that area *every day*. Doing the actual research gives us hard data to prove our estimate.

When you spend hours every day checking out the latest listings on the MLS, doing research on behalf of your clients, attending open houses, and analyzing sale data, it's hard *not to* become an expert on the local real estate market. The problem is that part time agents aren't doing all of the above. Or sometimes, *any* of the above.

You should know that in the Minneapolis area, there are a lot of part time agents. If I were interviewing agents, I would make sure to ask them a simple question: "Is real estate your career? Is it a full time job for you?"

You'd be surprised how many agents are simply dabbling in

real estate. They buy and sell a few properties a year. They're looking to make some extra cash. Or maybe they buy and sell their own investment properties, so they keep a license principally to have MLS access. Perhaps they're retired and just want something to do. Whatever their motivation, you should think long and hard before hiring someone who is part time. *Even if they are your relative.* (Ouch. Sorry. I had to say that.)

From my perspective, the part-time trend started in the late 1990s and 2000s as the housing market heated up. **During the housing boom, you actually *could* work part time and still make $40,000 a year (or more) as a real estate agent.** That's on top of whatever you were earning at your "real" job. With today's market, there are many *full time* agents earning that much. Or less. Oh, how times change.

Needless to say, those boom days of the last decade were crazy. Word spread that real estate agents were making a killing, and newly licensed agents started popping up like eager prospectors looking for gold.

Houses were selling like hotcakes—it didn't take much skill to show up to closings and sign papers. That may be an oversimplification, but it's not *too* far from the truth.

I think this time period is when people started to feel like real estate agents were making money *too* easily. And I can't blame them for thinking that.

Many homeowners started to silently wonder, "Wait, why am I writing you a commission check for twelve thousand dollars? You hardly did anything to market it! My home sold in eight days—that's fifteen hundred dollars per day!"

Today, many homeowners are *still* skeptical about the value provided by a real estate agent (which is why more and more people are trying to sell their home as a "For Sale By Owner"). I think this skepticism is a holdover from the days of the housing boom, when, to be completely honest, *that skepticism was justified.*

During the 2000s, it wasn't that hard to make six figures as a real estate agent. I personally knew agents that got their license and within two years were making over $100,000. Sometimes even in their very first year! There are not many professions where you can be a top income earner after two years on the job—and *little to no training.*

For the good part of the 2000s, the marketing plan involved three steps:

1. Upload new listing to the MLS
2. Place your sign in the yard
3. Sell it within a few weeks, show up to closing, collect commission check

It's not hard to see why people from all walks of life wanted to get in on the action! You could make millions as a real estate "investor" by simply buying a property in a nice area, holding on to it for a few years, and selling it after it had appreciated by 20%. This involved zero skill. *Anybody* could do it, and many people did.

It was like a game of hot potato—you just didn't want to be stuck holding an overvalued asset when the bubble popped. And eventually it did.

All good things must come to an end (for many of us who were personally *and* professionally affected by the housing bubble, we question whether it ever was a "good thing" to begin with).

Without getting into too much detail, low interest rates driven by the federal government's housing policy created an environment where *everyone thought houses would keep appreciating at astronomically high rates.*

Keep in mind that historically, real estate usually appreciates at the rate of inflation. If you look at long-term trends, owning a home is definitely not a get-rich-quick scheme. Unless, of course, you rode the housing bubble like a surfer on a good wave.

During the 2000s, homes were appreciating at five to ten percent per year! It was chaotic. And it created a casino-like approach to buying homes. Housing in the 2000s was like the California gold rush. The amount of transactions taking place was *incredible.*

Because people irrationally believed that the appreciation was permanent and their home would continue to increase in value by five to ten percent a year, they rushed to get home equity lines of credit (HELOCs) which borrowed against their equity.

In other words, many people were using their homes as cash machines.

If their home appreciated in value by ten thousand dollars in a given year, they would immediately go out and spend that as if it were real money they had earned. In reality, it was fake. It was paper wealth.

Many people used this money to go out and buy consumer products like boats, fancy cars, and expensive vacations. This wave of spending gave our economy a short-term boost that made it *feel* like everybody was wealthy.

In reality, **the entire housing market was being subsidized by the federal government providing easy money.**

The housing bubble had nothing to do with actual supply and demand, and everything to do with the federal government's monetary policy. The government had spiked the punch, and we were in for a nasty hangover.

Seeing an opportunity for "easy" money, many were lured into the real estate profession. They figured they'd get their license and get their piece of the action! And, well, I can't blame them.

During the housing boom, it was hard *not* to be making

money as a real estate agent. New listings would sell in days or weeks—not months. It was easy to get financing. RARELY did a sale collapse because of problems with financing. It seemed like banks were giving loans to anyone and everyone. Looking back, this was incredibly irresponsible, and a major reason why we had a boom and bust cycle in the housing market. I guess hindsight is twenty-twenty.

I've heard many people say that becoming a real estate agent is easy. And, again, on some level, they are probably right. It's really not that hard to take the classes, pass the test, and become an officially licensed real estate agent.

What *is* hard, and what separates amateur agents from the true professionals, is dedication to the industry.

You simply cannot develop expertise or market knowledge by spending ten hours a week or less.

Think about it this way: would you want your family's finances handled by a part time accountant whose real job is not in accounting?

Would you trust your investments to a part time financial

advisor who spends ten hours a week on the job?

Would you feel comfortable having your legal work taken care of by a part time attorney?

Would you be okay having a major operation done by a part time surgeon who just wants some extra spending money?

When the proper analogy is made, it seems *absurd*. Heck, I wouldn't want my hair cut by a part-timer much less buying or selling an expensive home!

Now, keep in mind all of these professions require proper licensing. Just like real estate, they do require official certification. But just because someone is licensed doesn't mean they are an expert. A piece of paper means they were smart enough to pass a test—it's *not* an indicator of true market knowledge, or wisdom that takes years to accumulate.

It might sound like I'm trashing part-timers. I am not. Some of them spent their lives in and around real estate, and now they are semi-retired. Not *all* part time agents are inexperienced or lack market knowledge; however, it's worth repeating the question I posed earlier: would you entrust **the largest investment you will probably ever make** to a part-timer for whom real estate is not their principal pursuit?

I mean, really, most people wouldn't hand over twenty thousand dollars to an inexperienced financial advisor, much less two HUNDRED thousand dollars!

When you pay the agent's commission, you are not paying for their time to help you fill out the paperwork at closing. To be honest, if you were willing to spend the time to read the documents thoroughly, you could probably figure them out by yourself.

The *real value* provided by a real estate agent is everything that happens up to that point. That is where it is invaluable to have a true professional—an expert—working on your behalf.

CHAPTER FOUR

WHAT YOU NEED TO KNOW *BEFORE* LISTING YOUR HOME

<u>Beware of agents that tell you what you want to hear in order to get their sign in your yard.</u>

There, I said it.

I realize that I may upset some of my colleagues by revealing this, but it needs to be said.

Sometimes what's good for the real estate agent is not what's good for the client.

Many folks mistakenly believe that their real estate agent always has their best interest in mind. And that makes sense, because if you read your average listing or buyer contract, it states that they/we are SUPPOSED to act in your best interest. That is part of what *agency* MEANS. But if we step back and look at the bigger picture, we can see how this does not always work out the way it ought to.

Let's examine a transaction from the real estate agent's perspective:

First of all, the main issue that real estate agents are struggling with every day is how to get more leads.

Sure, a typical commission for a real estate agent may be five thousand dollars (or higher, obviously depending on the price of the home), but that's not a lot of money if you're only doing four or five transactions a year. And many agents are indeed only doing that many.

The single most important issue for the average agent is the ongoing generation of business.

And, to be fair, this problem applies to every business. I'm sure that car dealerships, appliance stores, gyms, movie theaters, lawyers, insurance agents, restaurants, and every other business out there would appreciate more "leads" calling them. The problem is certainly not unique to the real estate profession.

But here's why it might be a more serious problem for real estate agents: ours is a feast or famine business. If you have a lot of prospects calling you, if you have multiple sales going on at the same time, life is good. Very good indeed.

But the reverse is also true.

Some agents sit at their desks all day praying for the phone to ring. Hoping that someone will call. If you are a real estate agent scraping by month to month, every transaction you are lucky enough to get is like a gift from above.

You may go a month without making a single penny, and then –*wham*- a six thousand dollar commission check. Of course, your margin is eroded pretty quickly after paying desk fees, broker fees, advertising invoices, spending hundreds a week on gasoline, oh and then there are the TAXES… but the point I'm trying to make is that this is a business which, for many agents, ebbs and flows.

Sometimes it's really good, lots of the time it's really bad.

For most agents, it's a more like hunting than it is farming. Farming is predictable. Farming is consistent. Hunting is not. Hunters may go days, even weeks, before they get the big kill. But then they can eat for days and days. And rest a lot, because they are tired and their stomachs are full.

Like the modern day real estate profession, hunting is feast or famine.

Here's another example:

If a small town used car dealer averages selling ten cars a month, it won't wipe out his business if he only sells nine. But if a real estate agent is selling one home per month, it can devastate them if a month or two go by without closing a sale.

(Keep in mind that most agents' desk fees, advertising budgets, auto expenses and so forth do not vary from month to month, even if no sales close.)

When your income comes in lump sums (commission checks) and not a steady, predictable stream of weekly paychecks that most employees are used to, an interruption in your income can wreak havoc on your personal finances.

In order to stave off such interruptions, it's VERY important for agents to cultivate a steady stream of leads. Because only a small percentage of all leads will ultimately become a paying client that buys or sells a home, agents need relatively large numbers of prospects to actually make a sale.

An agent might meet with five or ten people before one of them actually closes on a home.

I'm not telling you these things to bore you, or to elicit sympathy for real estate agents. I will show you why this insider information on how the business works is *very* important to know if you're thinking about engaging a real estate agent to represent your sale or purchase.

As I said: real estate is a feast or famine business. To be successful, it's extremely important to do everything possible to normalize the income stream. And that means drumming up leads from everywhere possible.

And one of the best ways to do that is to amass listings.

That's right. More listings. ANY listings.

The easiest thing a real estate agent can do to hedge against the uncertainty of an inconsistent income is to get more listings.

Real estate agents don't get rich by being expert marketers, or by having great service, or a fancy website, or by ensuring that your home sells quickly.

Real estate agents get rich by closing lots of transactions. But which ones? Maybe not all of them. You see, good listings generate OTHER business. They help agents get buyers (siphoned off from initial interest in a listing of theirs, but likely sold a totally different house,) and they also help agents get more sellers (your neighbors, perhaps?)

There are DOZENS of personal development books written for real estate agents. Maybe even hundreds. One thing they all have in common is a "get listings" philosophy. There are usually entire chapters in these books devoted to teaching agents how to accumulate more listings. In fact, there are *entire books* out there solely about getting listings.

At this point you're probably thinking, "How does getting a bunch of listings help a real estate agent get rich? Don't you actually have to *sell* your listings to make money?"

The answer is no.

<u>This is one of the biggest misconceptions about the real estate business.</u>

Many people mistakenly believe that agents are successful because they know how to market a property beautifully, or because they seem like such a good salesperson. Other people will tell you that the best agent is the one who is most networked.

(So there are plenty of agents out there desperately joining as many social clubs and organizations as they can, hoping to meet people and "network" their way to success.)

This is all well and good, but what success ultimately boils down to is getting listings.

I know, I know. It doesn't really make sense. After all, a used car dealer doesn't make money by accumulating a bunch of inventory. YOU HAVE TO ACTUALLY SELL CARS.

This isn't true in real estate.

Here's why: as soon as an agent signs a listing agreement and places their sign in that homeowner's yard, ANY agent can sell that home. Other agents have access to the MLS data, other agents can show the home to their buyers, and other agents can promote the home.

In fact, this is *usually* how it works. This isn't some weird exception or loophole in the rules. A vast majority of the time, a transaction involves a buyer's agent *and* a seller's agent.

In other words, the buyer and seller are *not* represented by the same agent. **Rarely does the actual listing agent find a buyer.**

What this means is that the commission is typically split two ways. The listing agent gets half and the buyer's agent gets half.

Because most of the work is done by the buyer's agent, collecting commission checks on your listings is *almost* a sort of passive income.

Notice I said *almost*. There is obviously work involved in listing a home and marketing that home, but it takes much more time working with a buyer than it does working with a seller.

Allow me to repeat that last sentence:

It takes much more time to work with a buyer than it does working with a seller.

Phrased differently, earning five thousand dollars of commission takes a lot more time to earn if you're representing buyers than if you're listing homes for sellers.

Working with sellers is a *scalable* business model.

In this way, increasing your income as an agent isn't linear; it can be exponential. However, if you are working with buyers, your production potential is limited. You can only work with so many buyers before you run out of hours in a day.

<u>This is not true of working with sellers.</u> Once they've listed with you and your sign is in the ground, you can start looking for the next listing, while waiting for another agent to bring a buyer for the last one.

Can you see how this creates a big incentive for agents to primarily pursue listings?

Oh, and did I mention that **having their sign in your yard is free advertising for the agent?** Newspaper ads in the local newspaper cost several hundred dollars per day. Billboards can be nearly one thousand dollars a month in prime locations. Radio ad campaigns cost hundreds of dollars per week. Sending direct mail is around fifty cents per letter. As you can see, advertising is expensive.

Don't underestimate the value to the real estate agent of having their sign in your yard for a few months. It's free advertising! And that is a big deal with how expensive most media has become in recent years.

When an agent has their for sale signs in dozens of yards, it's like having a collection of mini-billboards all over town.

This is yet another reason agents have an incentive to get listings. The ambitious real estate agent can *leverage their time* by focusing on working with as many sellers as possible.

When an agent focuses on working with sellers, they invest a little bit of time upfront in getting the listing, then the commission checks come in weeks or months later *almost as passive income.* Almost.

When you work with buyers, you are constantly spending time with them, touring homes, meeting with them, driving around researching neighborhoods, helping them arrange financing, and so on. Working with a buyer client is DEFINITELY not passive income for a real estate agent.

Don't get me wrong: I don't mean to say that it's bad for an agent to pursue listings. People need to sell their homes, and agents are here to list them.

But it can become a problem if the agent is singularly focused on getting listings *no matter what,* and not actually interested in seeing all of those listings sold. In other words, it's critical to discern whether an agent is doing their duty to pursue a seller's best interest (getting their house sold) or if they are just using the listing for free advertising to attract other clients.

Relatively speaking, collecting commission checks when you are the listing agent is passive income *when compared to representing a buyer.*

For most agents, their only time commitment once a listing contract is signed is calling to check in with the seller every week or so. Yes, there are open houses every now and then, but it's not like the agent is spending two hours every day on the front lawn jumping up and down waving their sign.

Working with buyers is *completely different*—it's easy to spend an entire afternoon with buyer clients, show them four houses, and not see any measurable return on that time investment.

I've had some buyer clients that I showed over TWENTY homes to before they ended up writing an offer. I tell you this not to complain about working with buyers. I LOVE working with buyers. It's *fun*! House-hunting in real life beats watching "House Hunters" on HGTV any day of the week.

But you need to know the incentives this system creates for real estate agents. On a per hour basis, it's MUCH MORE PROFITABLE to spend your time getting listings.

You can't scale or leverage your business if you're spending all your time with clients looking to buy a house. Real estate agents know this, so the savvy ones spend most of their time courting prospective sellers.

As you can see, this isn't necessarily what is best for sellers. To be fair, sometimes it doesn't matter. In a hot market, homes will sell regardless of which agent they are listed with, assuming the price is reasonable.

But you'd be shocked to discover how little time many agents will spend promoting your home *once they've got their sign in your yard.* Once it's uploaded to the MLS, they don't drop everything they're doing and start promoting your home. They simply move on to the next listing audition.

Making sales is important in real estate—but most agents focus on *selling the seller* on why they should list with them. Unfortunately, the actual marketing and selling of properties can often take a backseat.

Most agents don't do much to promote their own listings because they're too busy promoting *themselves* trying to get more listings.

I joke that for most listings, there is a three part marketing plan:

1. Upload listing to the MLS
2. Place sign in yard
3. Wait for somebody to call

If you're religious, there is a fourth step: Prayer.

All joking aside, the actual promotion of a property is usually quite minimal. Selling homes is very different from selling impulse purchases like food or clothing. Usually buyers who are already researching will contact you about the property. Effective marketing of a property certainly helps, but most of the time a listing is bought more than it is sold.

What I'm trying to say is that usually a successful transaction is more about the buyer buying the house than it is the listing agent selling the house.

It's not an impulse purchase that can be influenced by shady, manipulative, door-to-door style sales tactics…."So Bob, would you like to sign the papers today or tomorrow?" You can't trick people with "closing" techniques in real estate—it's a big purchase, and it won't be taken lightly.

The tactics that work to sell small dollar items don't apply in real estate. Sure, people's emotions come into play, but most people are smart enough to avoid spending two hundred thousand dollars on a whim.

Again, I'll repeat: **a successful transaction is more about the**

buyer buying than the seller selling.

This is one reason it's so crucially important to properly stage a home, fix what needs repairing, and price it right.

The greatest real estate agent in the world can't sell a home if it's ugly, broken, and overpriced.

I know, I know......*duh*. But you'd be surprised how many sellers blame their real estate agent for their home not selling when, in reality, the home was priced fifteen percent above the market and needed ten thousand dollars of interior renovations.

I could write an entire chapter about *that*, but I'll refrain from the digression for now.

There's an old sales proverb that says "Most people hate to be sold....but they love to buy."

Regardless of how effective an agent is at promoting and marketing their listings, it ultimately boils down to the question of whether there will be a match of willing buyer and willing seller, at a given price.

If there is, that buyer will find out about the listing one way or another, most likely either through an agent with whom they are already working, or through the internet. (This is one of many reasons that *For Sale By Owner* properties are at a disadvantage).

Now, you're probably wondering, "Gee Constance, I thought you placed a high value on marketing. It sure sounds like you're saying that marketing your listings isn't important."

All things being equal, the agent with a better marketing plan *will* sell more homes. But here's the thing: rarely are "all things equal." In fact, in real estate, things are almost NEVER equal.

There are all sorts of variables that can make a difference: price, days on market, motivation of seller, motivation of buyer, time of year, tax implications, relevant local sale data, staging, economic conditions, and so forth. I could rattle off a dozen more variables that can influence a sale, but I don't want to bore you.

The point is quite simple: when a home sells, the deal often happens because the buyer simply wants to buy. NOT because the listing agent *sold* it.

There is a difference.

Consider this:

Imagine you're waltzing through Target, looking for a new DVD that just came out. You ask a nearby sales associate where it is, and they tell you which aisle to find it in.

Did that employee sell you something? Not really—the purchase was driven by your willingness and eagerness to buy. You weren't "sold" at all. It's not as if you walked in to the store intending to buy shampoo, and the sales associate gave you a sales pitch ending with a hard sell, and you caved in and purchased the DVD.

Conversely, have you ever been to one of those timeshare seminars where they bribe you into attending with a gourmet meal and a moderately expensive free gift? *No one* goes into those meetings intending to purchase a timeshare.

But many do end up investing in the product being pitched.

These people truly are "sold." Because of an effective marketing strategy that persuaded them, they take action. The credit in this situation goes to the salesperson! They were "cold" leads, not intending to buy a timeshare.

This is not always true in a real estate transaction.

Once again, I'm NOT saying that listing agents don't do anything. I'm NOT saying you're better off trying to sell your home without an agent (FSBO). I'm NOT saying the real estate agent's commission is a waste of money.

But it's important for the home seller to understand how this works. Especially since your agent may gloss over the matter, if it comes up in conversation at all.

Successful real estate marketing is more about optimizing the home so that buyers want to buy it, and less about pouring tons of resources into promoting it.

Phrased differently, it's easier to sell a great product than it is to skimp on product quality, invest those dollars in marketing, and attempt to sell a mediocre product with a large ad budget.

Real estate agents understand this; most of the general public does *not*.

There's a reason that some agents have dozens (heck, sometimes more than fifty) listings at the same time. It would be downright impossible to work with that many buyers at the same time.

There wouldn't be enough hours in a day, or days in a week, to work with that many buyers.

Here's the secret: once you've done the up-front work of getting the listing, it's easy to sit back and hope another agent sells it.

In fact, many (though not all) agents put more energy and resources into getting listings than selling those listings. This is because they are still handsomely rewarded (with fifty percent or more of the commission) when another agent brings the buyer.

On a two hundred thousand dollar home, the commission will be roughly twelve thousand. This means that the listing agent would collect approximately half when another agent brings a buyer.

It's a much more scalable business model to simply rack up a bunch of listings and allow other agents to sell them. (Some firms do extra by hiring buyer's agents that work exclusively with buyers, and having marketing directors whose job it is to actually promote the listings.)

By avoiding spending time and resources promoting their inventory, brokerages can focus on generating as many listings as possible.

That's how it usually works behind the scenes.

Again, I'm not saying they don't spend *any* time marketing their listings. Just that it's much more profitable to get listings (not necessarily market them) and you'll usually see that reflected in how an agent spends his or her time.

This is different from other industries where you don't invest a lot of time or resources into selling individual units of inventory. However, with something as complex as a home, you need to become an expert on that specific property. It's not enough to be knowledgeable on homes *in general.*

As the listing agent, you need to know that specific listing inside out. You need to know its strengths, weaknesses, and how to answer questions, concerns, and objections. You need to become as much of an expert on that home than the homeowner him- or herself.

You need to commit to promoting each listing so that it sells quickly and for top dollar!

It's not the same as a car dealer having lots of inventory. In that scenario, buyers come to him. He doesn't go and prospect for buyers for the individual cars—he advertises the dealership itself.

Real estate agents can't (and shouldn't) do that—each of our products is unique. So, in my opinion, we should promote each of our listings as a unique product.

And THIS is where what's good for the real estate agent is *not necessarily* what's good for the client. It's not always a conflict of interest, but sometimes it can be.

Let's say you own some property in the Homewood neighborhood. After talking with a few neighbors, including some family friends that recently sold their home just up the street, you figure that your house is worth about three hundred thousand.

As it is for most Americans, your home is your biggest investment. You aren't really looking for a "quick sale" where you are forced to sell it below market value. You need every dollar you can get, and you're willing to wait for the perfect buyer who understands the true value of your home, and is willing to pay you what it's worth.

After interviewing several agents that want to list your home, you decide on Jake. Jake is a genuinely friendly guy, and his listing presentation was very impressive. To put the icing on the cake, Bob assures you that you can get three hundred thousand for your home.

Here's the problem: the market isn't willing to pay more than two hundred seventy-five thousand for your home. It's overpriced by about ten percent. This doesn't seem like a lot, but in Homewood, properties that actually sell usually go for about 95% of listing price, or higher. In some areas of the country, you can get away with overpricing a listing. But not here.

Most buyers don't want to risk offending sellers by offering what may be interpreted as a "low-ball" offer, even if the offer is actually fair relative to market value. In fact, many buyers would rather pass on the home entirely than take that risk.

By overpricing your home—even by a mere ten percent—Jake is virtually guaranteeing your home will not sell. In fact, it probably won't even receive offers.

Here's why Jake does this: HE WANTS THE LISTING.

Jake is willing to fudge the numbers a bit to massage your ego. He tells you *exactly what you want to hear*: that if you list with him, he can get you the three hundred thousand your home is worth.

Remember: you are not an expert on the local real estate market. You haven't spent hours researching sale data and creating a market analysis report. So what do you do? You listen to Jake. You trust him.

This is an example of *confirmation bias*, a term in psychology that describes a situation where people pretend to be objective. What's really happening is Jake told you what you wanted to hear, so you convince yourself that he's right. You didn't objectively analyze the situation, but instead you chose to accept the information that matched with what you *wanted* to be true.

In this scenario, the honest real estate agent that tells you the truth usually does not secure the listing.

When you hear that your home is actually worth two seventy-five, you don't want to believe it. Rather than confronting reality, what many sellers do is list with the agent that promises them the highest price. They don't know any better, so they substitute emotion for logic.

This dynamic can lead to some interesting listing presentations.

Oftentimes, the seller will get angry when you tell them what their home is actually worth. After all, the agent before you reassured them their home is worth *much more* than the number you gave them. By "low-balling" their home's value, you've insulted them.

I've had this happen to me more times than I can count—but it comes down to integrity. I believe a real estate agent should tell you what your home is actually worth—not what you *think* it's worth. Or worse, what you *want* it to be worth.

Oh, by the way, Jake knew this whole time that the home was actually worth about two seventy-five.

Here's another little secret of the real estate industry: creating market analyses reports is just as much art as it is science.

Sure, hours of research go into creating these reports, but the final recommended listing price is often influenced by the question of which number is going to resonate best with the seller, and therefore help the agent secure the listing.

Unfortunately, it's just a fact of life that human beings crave validation. We want to be told we're awesome. We want to be told our kids are awesome. And want to be told that our homes are worth lots of money. At least as much as our neighbors' houses. Or maybe a bit more.

Real estate agents understand this.

Real estate agents call this technique *buying the listing*. It's unethical, but there's really no way of proving that a real estate agent is doing it.

Let's go back to the example of Jake.

Because Jake succeeded in appealing to your ego, he wins the listing. Jake lists it slightly above three hundred, telling you he hopes to negotiate a final deal of three hundred, after allowing a margin of negotiation.

One month passes, and there have been two showings. No

offers.

The first month a listing is on the market is critical. If you aren't getting immediate attention in the first thirty days a home is listed—phone calls, emails, showings, offers—something is wrong with the listing. Nine out of ten times, it is overpriced.

Remember, Jake KNOWS it is overpriced. He quoted you a listing price that he knew was too high. After a few months of misery, Jake calls you up and tells you that, "The market has changed since we listed your property. Demand has dipped. Our original listing price is now too high. I think we need to drop the price twenty grand or so. If you are unable to do that, I understand. But I want you to know that with the current market conditions, I don't think your home will sell at the current price."

Jake will most likely quote you plenty of data to prove his point.

This is a technique commonly used by real estate agents. It shifts the blame from the agent to the market, so sellers don't get mad at the agent, when in reality, the agent *knowingly* overpriced the listing from the start.

A month passes, and you wait it out. You don't want to lose out on twenty thousand dollars, in case the perfect buyer comes along and falls in love with your house. But that doesn't happen. In fact, this never happens.

So, after multiple months of your home sitting on the market, you reluctantly give Jake a call and give him permission to drop the price of your home.

Voila—it sells within two weeks.

Most people (not knowing that the home was originally overpriced) will credit Jake with adapting to the market and doing what was necessary to get the property sold.

What usually goes undetected is that Jake uses this strategy over and over and over again to win listings from more honest agents.

Here's a breakdown of how some agents *buy the listing*:

1. Quote an inflated listing price to impress the sellers and get their foot in the door
2. Win the listing by convincing sellers the home is worth more than it actually is

3. Patiently wait while the overpriced listing accumulates "days on market."
4. When the seller's frustration reaches a breaking point, convince them to reduce the price (to the actual price it should have been all along)
5. Sell the listing months after it *should have* sold.
6. Repeat steps 1-5

This process is most easily executed when the seller agrees to a long-term listing contract. Sometimes it's as short as sixty days, but often the listing contract is six or even twelve months. Because the seller has signed a legally binding contract and cannot "fire" the agent, *they cannot escape*. The contract is what makes this underhanded tactic so effective—it doesn't really matter if the seller realizes he's been tricked, because the terms of the contract won't allow him to exit the agreement.

Agents know this, so most of them insist on the seller signing a lengthy contract.

Let me be loud and clear on this point: I DO NOT FORCE MY CLIENTS TO SIGN LONG TERM CONTRACTS. Period.

In fact, if a seller wants to fire me the day after they sign a listing agreement, I believe *it is their right to do so.* This incentivizes me to provide great service to all of my clients—if I don't, they can fire me with a quick email.

I call this my "Easy Exit Listing Agreement." To me, it's just common sense.

This raises an interesting question: why do so many agents insist on the seller signing a long-term contract? Are they that scared of their clients firing them, that they feel it's necessary to lock the client in to a contract?

To be fair, I'm not saying that all agents who use long-term contracts are evil. Not at all! I have *many* friends in the industry that use long-term contracts. So please don't take this out of context.

Contracts are not *inherently* a bad thing. It's when a contract is used as a tactic to take advantage of sellers that it becomes a problem.

In fact, historically, using contracts is a pretty standard practice in the industry. Most agents (and clients) sign contracts without thinking about it, because that's the way it's always been done.

Now that we've exposed how some agents buy listings, let's get into how to avoid this problem.

There are two HUGELY IMPORTANT questions you should ask *any* agent that wants to list your home.

First, "What is the average 'days on market' of your listings?" In other words, how long does it take you to sell your listings, on average? The answer to this question will reveal how quickly the agent sells their listings. Many agents out there can brag about selling the most homes in the area, or even getting "top dollar" for their clients—but it's all rather meaningless if it takes them 8 months to sell a home!

Here's why this is so important: asking the agent about their average *days on market* puts YOU in the driver's seat. You don't have to stress out about selecting an agent when you can *objectively* compare them based on hard data.

So feel free to ignore the fancy power-point presentations,

the glossy marketing literature, and the smooth talking sales jargon.

All that matters is the agent's track record of selling homes. And by that I mean *the actual MLS statistics*—not a vague reply like "Well I usually sell my listings very quickly!"

If the agent doesn't know their numbers (or refuses to give you this information), it's a pretty good indicator that you should *not* hire them.

In fact, many potential sellers are afraid of meeting with agents because they think the agent will give them an awkward hard sell they can't refuse. This is probably more of a problem in Minnesota….we are too "Minnesota nice" to politely refuse.

Again, the reason it's important to ask this question is because it puts *you* in control. Buying and selling a home is probably the most expensive thing you will ever do—doesn't it make sense to do some research?

Because, let's be honest, the reason it makes sense to hire a real estate agent in the first place is because you (the seller) aren't an expert on local real estate. But this is a paradox for many sellers—if you *don't* understand the local market, how can you possibly make an intelligent decision when it comes to choosing an agent?

Just like any other profession, there are agents out there that can give an amazing listing presentation, but fail miserably at actually selling houses. And the reverse is also true. There are agents that aren't particularly talented at wooing sellers, but are extremely effective at selling their actual listings.

So don't put too much emphasis on an agent's listing presentation. Take control of the situation and request the agent's average DOM statistic as part of the listing audition.

The second question you must ask is, "What is your average listing/sale price ratio?"

The answer to this question reveals how accurate the agent is at pricing their listings. *A good ratio is approximately ninety-five percent.*

Anything higher than ninety-five means the agent is selling their listings very close to the listing price. This is a good thing, because it usually attracts multiple offers and ensures the home sells quickly.

(Put another way, a ninety-five percent ratio means they are successfully selling one hundred thousand dollar listings for ninety-five thousand.)

Anything less than ninety-five means that they are chronically overpricing their listings. The actual target ratio will be different for every market. In some markets it may be ninety, or even eighty-five percent.

The higher a region's ratio, the greater the danger of overpricing your listing.

If there is a large difference between what an agent's list prices versus closed prices, you will know they are playing the "buy listings" game. Either that, or they're too inexperienced to know what local properties are actually worth.

Both of these are reasons to not hire this agent.

Remember to ask these two questions when it comes time to interview potential real estate agents. The very act of posing the questions (even if you don't get straightforward answers) puts you in control of the conversation. When you take the initiative in the listing interview, the real estate agent will think twice about trying to trick you with inflated numbers.

As they say, the best defense is a good offense!

And if you aren't personally selling anytime soon, *but know someone who is*, be sure to pass this advice on.

PS - The hypothetical story of Jake found earlier in the chapter is based on a true story. I changed the name of course, but the basics of the story are true.

I didn't get the listing because another agent convinced the sellers their home was worth much, much more than it actually was.

It took OVER ONE YEAR TO SELL.

And, for the record, I tracked this particular home. I was curious what it would end up selling for. Over a year later, it sold within two thousand dollars of the original listing price I had quoted the seller.

CHAPTER FIVE

DOES YOUR AGENT KNOW HOW TO SELL LUXURY HOMES?

I know what you're thinking already. You're like "Har-de-har Connie, this is supposed to be a book about *North* Minneapolis real estate. And there ain't no luxury properties on the Northside!"

Well, okay. I'll concede that to a point. But only to a point. The part I will concede is that we haven't yet seen prices that would widely be considered "upper bracket" in North Minneapolis. This is true. However, we DO have homes that rival Kenwood and Lowry Hill counterparts in quality of construction and detail. Please see Old Highland for the quickest (but not the only) example of that. Pick up a home on the 15XX block of Dupont Avenue North and move it to Kenwood, and we'll be looking at a value in excess of half a million.

I chose to make my home and business on the Northside because I see the potential. Urban living has regained its cachet, and people are moving back from the exurbs. The market is recovering, and there is only so much space in this city – only so many quaint older homes that today's young buyer can find within ten to twenty minutes of downtown. There are only so many such houses on transit corridors. And there are only so many such homes that exist in *neighborhoods* (the new catch-word the kids are using to indicate a place where they can walk or bike to things).

So there. Today's two hundred and fifty thousand dollar Old Highland Victorian is tomorrow's luxury listing. If you currently live in one, you know this to be true. (And in the meantime, I've been practicing on fine homes in South Minneapolis, so I know what it takes to get this kind of job done.)

So let's talk about high-end properties.

It sounds obvious, but the typical advertising used to sell a fifty thousand dollar fixer-upper will not work when marketing a million dollar mansion on Lowry Hill.

Many people mistakenly believe that all they need to do is spend a little more money to promote a "luxury" listing. They'll keep the actual advertising more or less the same, but simply buy more ads. Or larger ads.

But it is not that simple.

This isn't an issue of math, where you simply adjust the marketing budget to fit the listing price. Yes, you *will* need to invest more money promoting a luxury home. That's a given. Some agents fail to invest enough, which is their *first* problem. But it gets worse—some sellers make the wrong *kind* of marketing investments.

It's not as easy as taking whatever you typically spend on a normal listing and adding a few zeros.

If you want your luxury home to sell for top dollar in a reasonable amount of time, you can't settle for a difference *in degree*. You need a difference *in kind*.

I'm talking about the difference between evolution and revolution. Evolution implies you make minor tweaks to something. Revolution implies you completely start from scratch with an entirely new paradigm.

Effective marketing of luxury homes requires a completely different strategy. It demands an entirely new way of thinking. You can't just take the same advertising you use for regular listings, and buy larger ads.

I see real estate agents make this mistake all the time.

It is unfair to the sellers, because it virtually guarantees that their listing will sit on the market much longer than it should. And when a listing sits on the market for more than a few months, it begins to develop a reputation.

When buyers and their agents find a listing that's been on the market for a long time, they are more inclined to throw out lowball offers. And I can't blame them—it's a fair assumption that a seller may be desperate if their home hasn't sold after three, four, five months or more.

This creates a vicious cycle!

It's even worse for sellers of luxury listings, because instead of resorting to a price cut of five or ten thousand, they often are expected to trim the listing price by FIFTY or even one HUNDRED thousand.

In fact, I've seen high-end homes with long market time forced to undertake price reductions of greater than one hundred thousand! The higher the original price, the larger the reduction needs to be to stay competitive.

In real estate as in life, it's always in your best interest to make a great first impression.

And, like I said, this isn't an issue of math. It's about *psychology*. Affluent buyers that can afford high-end homes think differently.

Because affluent buyers think differently, they buy for completely different reasons than a typical homebuyer. Most homebuyers are concerned about details like utility bills and monthly mortgage payments. The luxury buyer does not care as much about these things, if at all.

The higher you move up the listing price ladder, the more important intangibles become. In other words, luxury homes are more about *art* than *science*.

On a typical one hundred and twenty thousand dollar starter home, the numbers drive the entire process for the buyer. The potential monthly mortgage amount, the utilities, the interest rate, and the closing costs are of high concern. Budget is a key driver of the process.

This is not true with luxury buyers.

Now, of course, affluent homebuyers still pay attention to *the numbers*. They won't allow themselves to get ripped off and over-pay for a home. If they were careless with money they probably wouldn't have become affluent buyers in the first place.

Instead of being limited by a strict budget, upper-end buyers generally make their buying decisions based on a completely different set of factors.

Affluent buyers are much more concerned about finding the perfect home than they are a home with the perfect *price*.

See the difference?

<u>Luxury real estate has little to do with price.</u> If an affluent buyer really, truly, wants a particular luxury home, they will pay for it. They want the perfect home, not the perfect price.

Affluent buyers are ruthlessly efficient in their businesses and careers *so they don't have to be when it comes to buying a home.*

I'm not saying luxury buyers don't care at all about price. *Of course they do!* Most affluent households still have an upper end to what they can afford. But within their budget, they have an entirely different conception of value.

They won't overpay, but they will pay *more*.

The average American earning $40,000 per year defines value as getting the cheapest price. Many of us associate the word *value* with brands like Wal-Mart or the Dollar Store.

Affluent buyers think of value not in terms of the cheapest price, but in *return on their investment*. And when it comes to buying luxury homes, the return they are looking for may not be financial. It may be emotional. They want to feel good about their home. They want to be proud of it. They may want others to be envious.

Not that the average American doesn't experience these desires—they just don't factor them into the home buying decisions. In a literal sense, they generally cannot afford to.

If you've studied psychology, you have probably heard of Abraham Maslow's *Hierarchy of Needs*. Maslow theorized that there is a pyramid of needs. We can only attempt to satisfy the "higher" needs once we've already satisfied the "lower" needs. At the base of Maslow's pyramid are basic physiological needs (air, water, food, et cetera). Once these basics are met, we then look for security. Once we've got *that* covered, we tend to pursue more abstract desires like social needs, such as friendships, family relationships, and the like.

At the top of Maslow's imaginary pyramid are spiritual desires like "achievement," "self-esteem," and "self-actualization." In a nutshell, once we have basic shelter and food on the table, we search for *meaning.* We want to be loved. We want to be appreciated.

In a very literal sense, buyers shopping in a lower price range may not worry about abstracts like self-esteem, achievement, or self-actualization (when it comes to buying a house).

Affluent people can afford to pursue these desires with their real estate purchases. And they do.

Stop and think about it: is any home really worth a million dollars? Certainly the labor and materials for much of today's new construction is not.

It's about *prestige*.

Paradoxically, the higher you move up the price pyramid, the less price matters.

From a purely marketing perspective, selling high-end homes is not about finding buyers.

It's about finding *a* buyer. Finding THE buyer.

In Minneapolis, there are many, many buyers out there for one hundred and fifty thousand dollar homes. Because of how many qualified buyers there are shopping in this price range, this is probably the easiest price point to sell a home. The "days on market" statistic for homes in this price range is much lower than in any other price range. There is plenty of demand!

And it also means these homes have to be competitively priced and positioned—if similar homes nearby are selling for one-forty, you can't afford to overprice your listing at one-fifty-eight. It simply will not sell—there are too many alternatives for buyers to look at instead. There is competition in this price range.

On the contrary, when it comes to high-end *luxury* real estate, the basic rules of microeconomics do not apply. The "supply and demand" rules you were taught in high school are next to meaningless. Why? Because all of these economic principles make an assumption that is NOT true in the luxury market: rational consumers engaging in *perfect competition*.

Price is merely one of many factors for affluent buyers. And, all things being equal, it's not a particularly important one.

Instead of science, it's art. Instead of mathematics, it's psychology.

And now that you understand the *why* of selling luxury homes, I will reveal the *how*.

Without giving away too many of my secrets, here are a few specific tips:

- High-end professional photography is a MUST. At lower price points, an agent might get away with taking their own pictures. The cameras on cellphones now are better than the digital cameras of just a few years ago—I see some real estate agents snapping property photos on their phones these days. This is unacceptable on a high-end listing. Engage a professional photographer to take the pictures. Yes, it will cost a lot more money. But if you are working with a real estate agent that refuses to invest a few hundred bucks into truly professional photos—on a listing that may generate a potential commission of twenty-five thousand dollars—you should probably find a new agent.

- When you write the property description, a simple list of the features is inadequate. Instead, a story should be told about the *benefits.* You may have heard the old advertising saying, "Sell the sizzle, not the steak." This is absolutely crucial when it comes to marketing luxury listings. Sell benefits, not features! Features are the desirable characteristics of a property—benefits take it one step further and describe why the characteristics are desirable in the first place, and specifically how the buyer's life will improve once they purchase the home. For example, we don't want to say, "This wonderful home has a full size, in-ground swimming pool." Instead, we should write something like, *"Imagine entertaining your friends on a hot summer day in your beautifully landscaped backyard—with an in-ground swimming pool! Instead of asking your neighbors if you can use their pool, be the family that other people have to ask. And if you have kids, they will love inviting their friends over for a day at the pool. Your pool, that is."* Can you see the difference? It's about illustrating through storytelling. The goal is to create vivid images in people's minds of how much better their life would be if they lived in this home. With lesser-priced listings, you might get away with simple descriptions of the floor-plan, the number of bedrooms, bathrooms, etc. Luxury listings demand more emotional, psychologically stimulating marketing.

- Create *targeted* buzz. We want to get word-of-mouth going about your listing! This can be done in a multitude of ways. Without revealing all of my marketing secrets, here are a few ideas:

- **Social Events.** Your agent shouldn't just hang out for 2 hours on a Saturday morning and hope people show up. Turn a luxury listing "open house" into a premiere social event that gets people talking! Have live music and finger-food (maybe hire a local chef or cater from a tasteful local restaurant). Yes, this will cost more money, but think in terms of value—not cost. Oh, and don't call it an open house. You want as many people to attend as possible, not just the relatively few affluent buyers that are currently shopping for a new home. You want the public to think of the event as a fun evening to look forward to, NOT an open house. The more people that attend your event, the better. Word-of-mouth is the goal. And don't promote the event to the general public—you want the affluent social circles to think of your event as *exclusive*, because it is.

- **Creative Direct Mail.** Again, the purpose of sending out direct mail is NOT to find a buyer. Very rarely, if ever, will someone get a promotional letter in their mailbox and subsequently decide to buy a million dollar home. Instead, the purpose of your mailer should be to drum up interest in the listing. Create some buzz! TELL A STORY about why this home is for sale, what a great opportunity it is, why the home is unique, etc. Don't focus on things like price, number of bedrooms, etc. The goal is to create an exciting mailer that piques people's interest—EVEN IF THEY ARE NOT CURRENTLY LOOKING FOR A NEW HOME. You want them to tell their friends at coffee about that interesting letter they received in the mail. Remember, when it comes to marketing a high-end luxury listing, we don't worry about finding buyers. We want to find THE buyer. There *is* someone out there that is a perfect match. The job of a real estate agent is to do whatever it takes to generate positive buzz and word of mouth in the community so affluent buyers know about the listing, even if they aren't looking to buy a new home. All it takes is one person to mention it to a friend who IS looking.

- **Online Marketing.** These days it seems like EVERYONE is online. Especially on social media. Most agents upload their listings to the MLS, and maybe aggregate them on a few of the online directories like Zillow and Trulia. I take it further, and a special website for each individual listing. That website will have a professionally photographed tour, so potential buyers can see the home from their couch. It will include a professionally written property description, and a way for interested buyers to contact me to find out more information. There is a certain amount of *prestige* when a property has its own unique website. I also use Facebook to promote my listings. I don't just post a link to the listing—I actively promote the listing with paid advertisements that my target market will see in their newsfeed. Facebook has a very robust advertising platform that some agents completely ignore! It allows you to target very specific demographics of people. I can't think of a good reason why you would *not* use social media to promote your luxury listings.

One last tip for owners of luxury homes: do not try to save money by refusing to update the interior of your luxury listing.

This strategy can work with lesser-priced homes, but it almost guarantees that a luxury listing will NOT sell. Or, even worse, it will sell at a bargain, *lowball* price.

If you have worn hardwood, *have it refinished*.

If your wall-coverings date to anywhere from the sixties to the nineties *replace them*. (*Unless your home is an impeccably-preserved mid-century modern specimen, in which case you should consult with an agent who knows historic properties before altering or updating anything – vintage can be valuable.)

If your appliances were brand new when you moved in 1997, *they are not new anymore*. Get new ones.

Buyers of luxury homes will not tolerate anything that is outdated**.** I mean, think about it: would you pay a half million or more for a home that will immediately require fifty thousand dollars of upgrades?

Again, the reason is not mathematical. It has nothing to do with price. Most affluent buyers that can afford a half a million dollar home could just as easily afford five-fifty. So it's not the extra expense of replacing old, outdated appliances, carpet, fixtures and so on, but rather the *convenience.*

Buyers don't want to worry about the stress and time involvement of managing an interior renovation. It's fun to watch on **HGTV**, but most people don't want that in real life.

If your home's carpets, appliances, countertops, fixtures, wallpaper, or paint colors are outdated, it's not their problem. It is *yours.*

Most affluent buyers are short on one thing: time. And trust me—they don't want to spend what little free time they *do* have shopping for carpets, wallpaper, or new appliances.

<u>It has nothing to do with the money.</u>

By definition, an affluent buyer can afford to buy all of these things, hire contractors to install them, etc. But this takes time. And if they have the option of buying a half a million dollar home that immediately requires fifty grand of upgrades to make it acceptable or buying a similar home that is newly updated and *move in ready* for five-fifty, guess which one they'll pick? They will choose the more expensive but turnkey home. Every single time.

In fact, *even if you discount the price of your home beyond what it will cost to make the necessary upgrades, it probably still won't sell.* Suppose you get multiple opinions and estimate that your home's outdated interior will need fifty thousand dollars of renovations. New stainless steel appliances, new carpet, new paint colors, stripping all the old wallpaper, and new fixtures.

If you don't want to deal with the nuisance of doing all this, remember this: <u>buyers won't want to either</u>. They'll simply pass on your home. Even if you discount the price by seventy five grand (which is twenty-five more than the fifty thousand of upgrades it requires), buyers will most likely *still* avoid your house.

When it comes to luxury listings, it's not about the math—it's about the psychology.

And the higher priced the home, the more this dynamic matters.

Discounting may work on a starter home. In a lower-to-moderate range, a ten thousand dollar compensatory reduction can attract an offer. A buyer might think the outdated interior represents a bargain opportunity. In this price range, buyers don't really expect stainless steel appliances, granite countertops, fresh contemporary paint, or an updated bathroom. They'd often rather save ten thousand on the purchase price than pay more for a newly upgraded interior.

<u>This is not true of affluent buyers.</u>

Rather than dealing with the stress of worrying about a potential renovation, upper-end buyers simply look at homes that are *already upgraded.*

They don't want to deal with wallpaper, paint, and other projects *for the same reason you don't* - it's time consuming and stressful.

If you know that a particular part of your home is outdated, fix it *before* you list the home for sale. If you don't, it may be a long, long time before your listing sells, or it may not sell at all.

CHAPTER SIX

SHOULD YOU SELL YOUR HOME WITHOUT AN AGENT?

For sale by owners have a reputation in our industry. Real estate agents typically refer to them by their acronym: FSBO, pronounced *fizzbo*.

As in the "fizz" created by soda pop, and "bow" used to fire arrows.

Anyway, there are two main reasons homeowners decide to sell their home **without** using a licensed real estate agent.

1. They want to save money on the commission because they feel they can do that part of the job themselves.
2. They originally listed their home with a licensed real estate agent, but were disappointed with the agent's performance.

Here's what you should know: over ninety percent of FSBOs eventually list with a licensed real estate agent. It's almost inevitable.

Why?

Sellers soon realize that selling a two hundred thousand dollar product (for example) is not as easy as pounding a sign into the yard and waiting for the phone to ring. And even in hot markets where that can work, it's almost a full time job responding to the phone calls, requests for tours, and miscellaneous inquiries. If the seller has a full time job or other time commitments, this makes things *extremely* difficult.

And in our modern age, I think a major reason that many homeowners try to cut out the middleman and avoid using a real estate agent can be summed up in one phrase: *the Internet.*

People mistakenly believe that homes are commodities. They think to themselves, "I'll just take a few pictures, write a paragraph or two about the features, upload it to a local *For Sale By Owner* website, and wait for the phone to ring!"

And then they wait.

And wait.

And wait.

The phone never rings. If it does, potential buyers are usually looking to score a great deal. They throw out low-ball offers. And I can't blame them.

Here's why: when your home is listed as a "For Sale By Owner," **the buyer knows that there isn't a middleman.**

They feel that *they* are entitled to some of that extra profit—not you, the seller. So typically they make lower offers than they otherwise would. This practically eliminates any hypothetical savings that may have been realized, presuming that the home is lucky enough to attract any offers to begin with. In fact, many homes listed without an agent fail to attract a single offer.

When this inevitably happens, the seller gets frustrated, and understandably so.

Eventually, he or she will probably end up listing the house with a licensed agent.

I won't beat around the bush here. I firmly believe it is in your best interest to buy and sell real estate with an experienced, licensed agent, preferably a certified Realtor.

SECTION TWO

FOR BUYERS

CHAPTER SEVEN

CHOOSING THE REAL ESTATE AGENT THAT IS RIGHT FOR YOU

Buying a home is one of the most complex and expensive purchases you will ever make, and it's not a purchase I would recommend making without the assistance of a professional.

Unless you have direct experience in the real estate industry, it will be extremely hard to wing it.

And even if you have experience in real estate, you are still putting yourself at an extreme disadvantage by not being represented by a licensed agent, preferably a *Realtor*.

To avoid making expensive mistakes, you have to understand our local market, know where the inventory is, what the short term and long term trends are, how to negotiate, what contracts and inspections to perform, how to effectively market your listing or efficiently search for your new home. The time you have to invest can cause you to pull out your hair if you don't know what you're doing.

Nearly ninety percent of *for sale by owners* eventually list their home with a licensed real estate agent. Why? Because in time, they figure out it's a lot harder than it looks. Specifically, a lot more time consuming.

There is a reason we hire real estate agents. But which should you choose? What should you look for in an agent? It's not an easy choice, but here are five things you *should not* do and five things you *should* do.

1. *Don't* choose the first agent you meet

Let me ask you a question: would you marry the first person you met? Of course you wouldn't. The same logic applies when it comes to choosing a real estate agent, even if the agent is a referral.

While it's not a long-term commitment like a marriage, buying or selling a home can be a huge, high-stress endeavor (if you don't believe me, ask anyone who has bought or sold real estate). You want to make sure you've picked the *right* person to help you navigate those waters. (And that right person might not be me, for the record.)

I'm not writing this book to convince you that *Constance Vork is awesome and all the other agents are terrible.* Instead, I hope this book is a valuable resource that empowers you to ask the right questions and make a more informed decision. I wish I had a copy of this book back when I first started buying and selling homes over fifteen years ago.

Here's the bottom line: we have some amazing, highly professional agents here in North Minneapolis. I want to make sure you pick the agent that is right for *you.*

Get as many recommendations as you can, and take the time to interview several real estate agents. Ask each agent questions like these:

- Are you a member of the National Association of Realtors?
- Will you show me houses in all the neighborhoods I ask for?
- How familiar are you with the area?
- How long have you been in real estate full time?
- What is your average list price to sale price ratio?
- What is the average DOM (days on market) of your listings?
- What is your strategy/plan to help me find a home?

- Do you work weekdays and weekends?
- What makes you an expert on local real estate?
- Why should I choose you over other agents?

Compare the answers with your other interviews, and choose an agent who best matches your personality, style, and goals.

It's sad, but most people do more research on what car they want to drive than what real estate agent they work with. While car shopping, they'll do research online, physically go to a few dealerships, take a few test drives, compare and contrast, *then* they make a decision.

Very few people do this when it comes to buying or selling homes. They just call the number on a yard sign, or take a blind recommendation from a friend without doing any research.

Trust me. You will be much happier with your buying or selling experience if you are happy with the agent you chose. Take your time and pick the right one.

2. *Don't* hire someone just because he or she says what you want to hear

You want an agent who will challenge you. And agent who will tell you when you are wrong. You want an agent who will keep you from making a huge financial mistake. Many agents are so concerned with not offending their clients that they are afraid to be blunt with them. To me, this is critically important. You are engaging a professional for their expertise. If they don't provide that, what's the use of hiring them?

If I were a buyer or seller, I would want an agent that was absolutely *brutally honest* with me.

It's one thing if a retail associate at Target or Best Buy sugarcoats a product, telling you what you want to hear to massage your ego. If you end up making the wrong decision on a fifty dollar swivel chair, life goes on. But when it comes to the biggest investment of your life, don't you want to know exactly what you're getting into?

Agents that are not brutally honest are doing you a HUGE disservice. They are afraid the client will get mad and fire them. Well, I would rather you fire me because I gave you honest advice (that may have temporarily offended you) than watch you make a mistake that costs you a lot of money. In addition to the fact that I genuinely care about my clients' futures, my reputation is on the line.

I can't afford to let my clients make expensive, preventable mistakes. And they *definitely* can't afford it!

Look for someone who is assertive but not obnoxious. Ask him or her how they would respond if you wanted to make an offer on a house they knew was way beyond your budget, make a lowball offer in the wrong situation, or any other ethically difficult situation.

A good agent does what is right, and looks out for *your* wallet, even when that's not good for theirs.

3. *Do* Work with a Buyer Agent

Did you know that all real estate agents are deemed to be working for the seller *unless* there is a written agreement that says otherwise?

That's why a *Buyer Representation Agreement* is a smart move for anyone in the market to buy a home. There really aren't any exceptions to this. It is ALWAYS in your best interest to work with a buyer agent that is representing *you*—not the seller.

Buyer's agents come in a few flavors:

General Buyer Agent: Many real estate brokerages have designated buyer agents that primarily work with buyers. These agents usually don't have a lot of listings, so the potential for conflict of interest is a bit lower. Any agent or broker, however, can enter into a *Buyer Representation Agreement* with you to help you find a home and protect your interests.

Accredited Buyer's Representative: The ABR designation signals that an agent has taken advanced courses specific to buyer representation, and along with meeting other requirements has been accredited for working specifically with homebuyers.

Exclusive Buyer Agent: Exclusive buyer agents never work for sellers, because they don't take listings and neither does the brokerage they work for. Instead, these agents work *exclusively* for buyers.

This is the only form of buyer agency that completely eliminates a conflict of interest between your agent/broker and the seller.

If you're working with anyone other than an exclusive buyer agent, the possibility exists that you will want to buy a listing that is held by the agent you're working with or the brokerage firm that agent works for. This is a situation called *dual agency*, and it means that the seller has already received the bulk of the guidance from the brokerage, but your representation might become more neutral.

Now, let me be very clear. I don't want you to misunderstand what I'm saying here: *there is absolutely nothing illegal or unethical about dual agency.*

The only potential problem is that a real estate brokerage is put in a situation where it has to balance loyalties between both parties, which can lead to some sticky negotiating situations.

Sometimes a real estate agent working on a "dual agency" transaction will lower their commission, slightly (I'm actually not allowed to publish commission rates—contact an agent for specific details).

Again, this is not required by law, but you should know that it's a somewhat common practice.

The buyer's rep agreement doesn't have to be in writing, but it does show that the process and commitment have been thoroughly explained. You CAN ask for representation and receive it *even if you aren't willing to sign the contract.* But don't expect that an agent will remember you or what you need, which may allow a more committed buyer to get YOUR dream home.

Make sure there is an escape clause in your contract so that you don't get trapped into a long-term agreement with an agent you dislike. Personally, I always have flexibility with my clients and contracts. I don't want them to feel pressured into signing or agreeing to *anything.*

4. *Don't* hire agents who don't know how to negotiate

The real estate industry is full of part time, inexperienced real estate agents. These are the last people you want to help you buy your new home, and a good reason why you should choose a member of the *National Association of Realtors*.

But even for those who have made it a full-time career – and thoroughly enjoy what they do – if they are afraid of conflict and don't have sharp negotiation skills, they are not going to maximize your experience.

Look for a real estate agent who's not afraid to make tough requests or knows how to deal with a low-ball offer.

5. *Don't* hire agents with abnormally high numbers

Every market has real estate *superstars*—agents that have figured out how to leverage their time and money so that they can generate millions in annual sales.

But you might not want to hire them.

That could sound counter-intuitive. You are probably thinking: *Wouldn't a superstar be a superstar precisely because they are a fantastic agent?*

Well, no, not really. You see, a super-successful agent may or may not have what you are looking for. You and that agent may also define success very differently.

One agent may define success by the number of transactions he closes a month, the amount of commission he makes, the number of awards he's accumulated.

Another agent might define success with the number of healthy relationships she's built, satisfied clients she has, or the number of testimonials she receives.

One agent is all about himself. The other is all about you. Choose the one who is in alignment with your personality and goals.

Again, I'm not saying that superstar real estate agents are to be avoided altogether. If they have high transaction numbers, *clearly they know what they are doing.* But you need to know what you're getting into! You don't want to be an anonymous number in their sales statistics.

And to achieve high *production* numbers, it's almost impossible to dedicate yourself to each and every client.

If an agent is all about *their* goals, it's hard for them to focus on *yours*.

Find an agent committed to *you*.

6. *Do* choose an agent who deals with your price range

To most non-experts, selling a home seems pretty straightforward, whether the home costs fifty thousand or five million. But the truth is, you should choose an agent who is an expert in your price range.

Just as doctors specialize, so should real estate agents. Price ranges will vary from market to market, but in Minneapolis you could probably break them down into:

- Under $100,000
- Over $100,000 but under $300,000
- $300,000 and higher

You should also look for agents familiar with the type of purchase you are considering, as there are differences in the process for things like condos, second homes, luxury properties, and transactions that involve relocation companies.

And, of course you should also choose an agent who is an expert in the area you want to live. For example, if you want to look at homes in North Minneapolis, don't be surprised if an agent from Southwest Minneapolis has zero interest in showing them to you. Or if they are willing, they might not know the difference between Victory and Old Highland.

If you're unfamiliar with the area, you will not be an effective agent. Period. If you are interviewing agents, ask them if they are familiar with the specific neighborhood or area of town you plan on buying or selling in.

7. *Do* pick an agent who fits with your personality

Good real estate agents approach the art of buying and selling houses differently because they know that each client is different in personality and needs. Some agents even specialize in dealing with particular client types.

In her New York Times article *Who's Got Your Back?* Vivian S. Toy identifies four such real estate agents:

- **Hand-Holder** – This person will be slow to speak, slow to make a move, and will be patient when you have a thousand questions to answer. He won't mind answering the same questions ten times. He understands the anxiety behind buying a home and will help you calm down.

- **Authority** – This person is loaded with knowledge about the market and inventory, understands the ins-and-outs of real estate, and is confident in that knowledge and experience. He is a take-charge type.

- **Team** – This is a group of people who specialize in certain aspects of real estate, usually led by an authority (the face on all the promotional material). This team is on call at all hours – an efficient and effective, well-oiled machine. The only downside is you will never work with the person you met on your introductory visit, if you met him at all.

- **Legacy Broker** – This person is someone who has been the go-to person in a certain family or social circle. She values the relationship with the larger group, so you know she won't steer you wrong. However, this kind of agent is difficult to find ... and it can be hard to get inside that inner circle.

These categories aren't definitive. Every agent is probably a mixture of each. But hopefully this gives you a *general* idea of how agents can have different personalities and approaches.

Personally, I would say I'm probably more of the *authority* type, with a little *hand holder* mixed in when I'm dealing with clients that have lots of questions, such as first time homebuyers.

8. *Do* choose a full-time REALTOR

When it comes to buying or selling a home, you want an experienced, professional real estate agent by your side. As I've said elsewhere in the book, you want an agent that eats, breathes, and sleeps real estate. Don't settle for a part-timer, and don't be someone's on-the-job-training!

Full time agents have a few distinctive traits that set them apart from part-timers.

- They are career real estate specialists
- They will work to lower your risk
- They will work for you at their own risk
- They understand the current market
- They have and know inventory
- They understand the complexity of the transaction

- They have *wisdom* versus just *knowledge.* Wisdom is the ability to apply years of knowledge. A rookie can have knowledge if they read a few books—it takes an experienced Realtor to truly have market **wisdom.**

In addition, look for agents with some additional training. Having various certifications doesn't guarantee an agent will be right for you (or even a good agent at all) but it at least shows that they are dedicated to professional development.

You'll know this when you see the weird acronyms behind their name. Here's what some of those acronyms mean:

- **CRS (Certified Residential Specialist)**: A network of thirty-three thousand agents who receive tools and training to help buyers or sellers make the residential transaction as smooth as possible.
- **GRI (Graduate Realtor Institute)**: According to National Association of Realtors' website, GRI designees: *Have pursued a course of study that represents the minimum common body of knowledge for progressive real estate professionals, have developed a solid foundation of knowledge and skills to*

navigate the current real estate climate (no matter what the market condition), and act with professionalism and are committed to serving their clients and customers with the highest ethical standards.

- **ABR (Accredited Buyer's Representative)**: Another designation that signals to buyers that a real estate agent is serious about honing their skills.
- **Certified *Realtor***: Many people mistakenly believe the term "Realtor" is synonymous with real estate agent. It is not. According to the NAR's website, *the term REALTOR® is a registered collective membership mark that identifies a real estate professional who is a member of the NATIONAL ASSOCIATION of REALTORS® and subscribes to its strict* **Code of Ethics**.

The Code establishes time-honored and baseline principles that come from the collective experiences of REALTORS® since the Code of Ethics was first established in 1913. Those principles can be loosely defined as:

- *Loyalty to clients;*

- *Fiduciary (legal) duty to clients;*

- *Cooperation with competitors*

- *Truthfulness in statements and advertising*

There are many other designations and acronyms. Everything from resort specialists to working with senior citizens. If there is a niche market, it's safe to say there is probably a professional certification with an acronym.

While agents *without* designations can be as superb as those *with* the designation, one thing you know that you are getting with an agent who has additional designations is a commitment to excellence and professional growth.

9. *Do* ask friends for referrals

Getting recommendations from friends is an essential step in finding a great real estate agent. But when asking, be very specific. This is where most people go wrong in seeking referrals. Be extremely specific about what you are looking for in an agent! A simple question like, "Do you know any good agents?" is too vague.

What your friends and family like in a real estate agent *may not be what you like*. To evaluate a recommendation, ask your friend or relative a few additional questions:

- What about this agent do you like?
- What was your experience working with this agent?
- What didn't you like about this agent?
- What do you wish they had done differently?

If you like what you hear, jump on the real estate agents' website and find out as much as you can about them. Feel free to visit them at an open house.

10. *Do* choose an agent who responds to you

How soon did he return your call? Did he return your call at all? Does he respond to text messages, emails, social media, or blog comments? For how long? This may seem minor, but how soon and how often an agent responds to your communication will tell you a lot about who he is and how he works.

Keep in mind that some agents will put their best foot forward when first meeting, so first impressions may be deceptive.

Ask for some references, and then follow up with them to see what they thought about the agent's responsiveness.

One more thing—remember that YOU are in the driver's seat. YOU are in control. YOU are buying or selling a house, not the real estate agent. Don't let the real estate agent's agenda get in front of yours.

CHAPTER EIGHT

THE FIFTEEN MOST COSTLY MISTAKES MADE BY HOMEBUYERS AND HOW TO AVOID THEM

1. Lack of Vision

You cannot depend on your eyes when your imagination is out of focus.

-Mark Twain

When I first got involved with real estate fifteen years ago, I went in with the assumption that other people saw the same thing that I saw when we looked at properties. I thought that everyone would share my delight at natural woodwork, high ceilings, and gingerbread detail, even on a vacant and boarded property with burst pipes and a little-bitty vermin problem. I figured that everyone would see such a property for what it could be... what it *should* be.

Have you ever watched one of those reality TV shows about home renovations? "Property Brothers" on *HGTV* is one of my favorites. The basic idea of every episode is two brothers (one is a contractor, one is a Realtor) attempt to convince someone to buy a fixer upper, and spend the difference on an extensive renovation budget.

For example, instead of buying a two hundred thousand dollar house, you purchase an ugly, outdated home that needs lots of repairs for one-forty, and then spend the extra sixty turning it into your dream home.

Usually the buyers start out incredulous. The property brothers try to convince the buyer that this *is* their dream home - it just needs some work. The buyer is skeptical that a house *this ugly* could ever be brought up to the level of the move-in-ready counterparts. In short, they have no vision.

Obviously, what happens is the property brothers and their crew renovate the ugly house into a magnificent home. Their vision allows them to see potential in ugly houses. And that's the big idea here: the key is the potential.

Sure, there are properties out there which are simply horrendous. There's no other way of saying it. And North Minneapolis definitely has its fair share of these homes. But for the buyer who's willing to get his or her hands dirty, any one of those properties can equal a serious opportunity.

Instead of buying a home that's move in ready, consider buying a cheaper property home that's cosmetically ugly and needs some repairs. Invest the difference in a custom renovation that will turn a bargain fixer-upper into your own dream home.

Remember: cosmetic problems are usually the easiest and most affordable fixes. Older kitchen cabinets, appliances, carpets, and paint are not terribly expensive to replace. In fact, you might be surprised at how far ten thousand dollars can go.

In many cases, you can *completely transform* a home with as little as ten thousand dollars' worth of cosmetic upgrades.

This gives you a massive advantage as a house hunter. It means you can research many more homes than the average buyer, because you aren't confining your search to the relatively few homes that are truly move in ready.

When you have vision, you have more options. And when you have more options, you have leverage during negotiations. And leverage is a very good thing.

Besides, *move in ready* is a pretty subjective concept. Everyone has a different tastes in interior design, layout, and so forth. Even on a home you originally think is perfect, you'll most likely change things.

Most of these ugly properties are usually passed by because buyers are so obsessed with homes that are move in ready. As you know, homes that are really, truly, *move in ready* almost always have a premium price.

What this means for you is that if you have the patience and creativity to see the potential in a home, you can score a bargain. Not that many owner-occupant buyers are willing to look at outdated homes. And if they are, these examples often propel them right to the houses at the top of their price range, as they compare how nice those more expensive home look, feel and smell!

It never even occurs to them that they could purchase an outdated or ugly home at a steep discount, and have plenty of money left over to completely renovate it into their dream home.

The vast majority of house hunters only see the product that's there *right now.* They see the dirty carpets, peeling paint, old or missing appliances, or the poorly maintained yard. *People with vision see none of this; they see opportunity.*

2. Ignoring The *One Thing* You Cannot Change

Rather than being concerned with cosmetics, here's the one thing you should *not* compromise on: location.

The old saying, *location, location, location* should be your top priority. It's a cliché for a reason!

Why? Location is the one thing you can't change.

This is a pretty profound insight: you can change ANYTHING about a house, *except location.* So when you find the right house in the perfect location, remember that anything and everything you don't like about it can be remedied.

Here is an example that illustrates both the vision and the location concepts:

I was working with a young couple that were relocation from New York City to Minneapolis, and they had a pretty tight budget, which ultimately led them to North Minneapolis. (Funny how that works – I see this all the time – buyers start out not wanting to consider the Northside, but then change their minds when they see what their money will get them there versus on the Southside.)

Ben and Sarah were the buyers' names, and Sarah's father was a contractor. He had built his own home with his bare hands, and was clearly eager to help them with their future home. They, on the other hand, were less enamored with the idea of a fixer.

These buyers were hoping to spend about one hundred thousand dollars on their future home. Now, in 2012 when we were shopping, there was very little available in that range. In fact, North Minneapolis was their ONLY hope of finding a home of that price.

But recall that North Minneapolis is a large area – there are thirteen different neighborhoods inside of it and the mini-markets that they constitute can vary greatly.

One of the more sought-after neighborhoods over North is Homewood. Its proximity to Theodore Wirth Park, graciously-designed housing stock, and relatively stable population with a low rate of rental makes it appealing to a great many buyers.

We found a GREAT brick Craftsman house in Homewood. Actually, we found TWO, but one in particular seemed perfect for them. It was rough around the edges, to be sure. It needed floor-sanding, fresh paint throughout, and it had a pretty dated (but still usable) kitchen and bath. It had an older roof that would likely have needed replacing within a few years. But it was just under one hundred thousand. And it was in HOMEWOOD. Nearby properties that were in good shape were listing fifty to one hundred percent higher.

Alas, the buyers felt overwhelmed by the relative dinginess of the interior (I should add that the house was bank-owned, so it was also dirty and had had zero attempts made by the listing broker to present it in its best light) and they decided to pass on it. It sold very soon after our showing.

Ultimately, the buyers ended up going with a home in the Hawthorne neighborhood that had been rehabbed by a non-profit organization. Sarah's father gave them extra money so they could afford the price, which was fifty percent higher than what they had originally budgeted.

Ben and Sarah were happy for a while. But then guess what happened? The employer for which they both worked (and which had brought them to Minneapolis in the first place) decided to move them again, two years later. And guess what else? Hawthorne is one of the least stable Northside neighborhoods, and has shown the slowest appreciation rate over the last several years. So Ben and Sarah's one hundred and fifty thousand dollar house has NOT appreciated in value, but they need to leave anyway. And they cannot sell it without taking a loss.

I wish I had succeeded in convincing them to go with the Homewood fixer instead.

Ben and Sarah broke one of the cardinal rules of real estate: it's always better to buy the worst house in a nice neighborhood than the nicest house in a challenged neighborhood. *

LOCATION, LOCATION, LOCATION.

And a little vision doesn't hurt, either.

*I don't mean to pick on Hawthorne, for what it's worth. I have personally bought two houses in that neighborhood, and am very glad

I did so. However, the two houses TOGETHER cost me less than forty thousand dollars.

3. Failure to Interview *Multiple* Agents

There is a secret about buyers that most real estate agents know and capitalize on. That secret is that buyers typically work with the first agent who offers to help them find a home. They might meet this agent through a referral, or at an open house, or, in some cases, because this agent has a house listed that the buyer is interested in.

Imagine that you're out driving around on a Sunday afternoon looking at homes. You find a home that you really, really like. It's in the right neighborhood, and the yard has excellent curb appeal. Naturally, you want to find out more!

You decide to call the agent whose sign is in the yard. You meet with that agent, because you think they are the only one who can show you the house.

This is incorrect.

And that agent, for the record, represents the *seller*.

Not you.

Nowadays, most agents are part of the MLS (multiple listing system). That means that any of us can show almost any property out there.

So, before you call a total stranger from off of a lawn sign, consider your various options.

(One reason agents love getting listings is that yard signs generate lots of phone calls. The more yard signs they have, the more leads they get.

Friends, I beg of you: before making what will probably be the largest financial decision of your life, interview some agents. Or at least talk to a couple of people who know the area, and see if they have recommendations.

Now, I'm not saying you should automatically hire *me*, Constance Vork. Don't get me wrong—I would love to have the opportunity of working with you. Maybe we'd be a great fit! I sure hope so. But you should *always* do some research before hiring a real estate agent. It's a big decision.

I don't know of any businesses that hire the first person that applies for a job. Nope, that's not how it works. Often times the competition for job openings is fierce. The company's Human Resources staff will sort through resumes, and choose only a handful to actually come in for an interview. *Only then will they select the very best candidate.*

Don't you think you should put a little thought into who *you* hire?

ALWAYS, ALWAYS, ALWAYS ask for testimonials.

Testimonials are the best kind of research you can do. Take everything the agent says with a grain of salt. *Of course* they'll say good things about themselves. And that goes for me, too! Don't take my word for it - check out what my clients are saying about me!

Make sure the agent you pick *knows the market.* Real market wisdom takes years to hone. Don't be someone else's learning curve. Here are some questions to keep in mind:

- Are they local?
- How long have they lived in your area?
- Are they full time?

- Do they have advanced credentials? (There is a difference between *Realtors* and real estate agents)
- Do they come across as trustworthy?
- Are they able to answer your questions without hesitation?

4. Not Being Prepared for Multiple Offers

The last several years have been filled with news stories (and cocktail party stories, and water-cooler stories) about the down market, lingering inventory, upside-down homeowners, and other tales of doom and gloom. Luckily though, the media is finally catching up to what real estate agents and active buyers have known for more than a year now – and that is that the sellers' market is returning.

In a sellers' market, there are less available homes than there are willing buyers. This phenomenon cycles back and forth with its opposite (that being the rut we just pulled out of) where there are many more houses than there are interested buyers.

Right now inventory is low. But since we're on the front end of a housing recovery, prices are also still somewhat low. The result of that mix is that we have properties getting multiple offers in very short periods of time.

One question I hear regularly from buyers is "how do we know the agent isn't lying when they tell us there are other offers?" This is a very good question indeed, and it's one I've asked my own agent in the years prior to becoming a licensed Realtor. The answer is hard though. We can't know for sure. But we have to trust them, because agents are not supposed to lie.

Besides being aware of the chances of ending up in a multiple offer scenario, the best thing you can do to prepare for it is to listen to your agent. They should know the market well enough that they can predict many of the properties that will go into multiples quickly. This is because the agent knows what most houses are selling for, and how a given property compares. (Again, here you see the benefit of working with an agent who is full-time, and experienced in their market!)

Another thing you can do to prepare is to keep your top dollar amount in mind, and keep in touch with your loan officer, if you are financing the purchase. Everyone is impacted differently by competition. Some shy away from it, and some are energized by it. You want to make sure that a) you don't lose an opportunity by *not* bidding, but also b) that you don't get swept up in the moment and overpay, just because you want to be the winner.

5. Losing Money by Ignoring the Power of Negotiation

In business as in life, you don't get what you deserve, you get what you negotiate.

–Chester Karrass

Earlier, we touched on *location, location, location.*

Well, there's another word you need to commit to memory: *negotiate, negotiate, negotiate!*

To avoid leaving money on the table, you'll need an experienced agent who understands the art of negotiation. For the most part, the skill of negotiating is something that is developed through experience. Like most things in life, the more a person does it, the better they become.

And that brings up an important question: **how are you supposed to develop the skill of negotiation when you will probably**

only buy or sell a few homes in your lifetime?

The answer is simple: you need to trust the experience of your real estate agent.

I have participated in hundreds of negotiations, both in buyers' markets and in sellers' markets. I have represented both sides of the table: buyers *and* sellers. When you consider how many transactions I've been involved with, you can probably guess that I've seen nearly every type of negotiating tactic, and had the opportunity to respond on behalf of my clients.

It *pays* to use an expert.

Consider this:

Most people think that attorneys (another profession based upon representation of a client) make pretty good money, and generally that is true. Let's say for example's sake that the average attorney bills two hundred dollars per hour. At that rate, it would take twenty-five hours to generate five thousand dollars of pre-tax income. So a lawyer has to work twenty-five hours to earn (or save) five grand.

For a home buyer in Minneapolis buying a one hundred and

fifty thousand dollar home, you and your agent could "earn" you five thousand in two hours of negotiations.

That's *twenty-five hundred* dollars per hour.

If you are buying a home, and you negotiate that the seller pays your closing costs, that can *easily* add up to five grand.

Or maybe you can get them to lower their price by twenty-five hundred and agree to cover the same in closing costs. If that works, you just earned five thousand dollars! EVERYTHING is negotiable. The appliances, artwork, furniture, closing costs, home inspection, moving expenses, you name it. It all depends on your creativity.

Keep an open mind, and find a win-win situation!

You should know that the more expensive the home, the easier it is to "make money" during negotiations. On higher priced luxury homes, it's not uncommon for people to negotiate in twenty-five thousand dollar increments.

"I'll give you $650,000."

"Nope, I need $715,000."

"Well, how about $675,000?"

"Could you do $690,000?"

When you really stop and think about it, this is *amazing*. The average American earns around thirty thousand dollars per year, and in many real estate transactions that much money can be made or lost in a split second decision. And it all depends on how skilled you are at negotiating.

For the average person, there is no easier way to earn money than developing solid negotiation skills. Period.

And if you aren't the type of person that feels comfortable negotiating, this is yet another reason why it's so important to work with a real estate agent you *trust*.

In many situations, a real estate agent can save you more money during negotiations than you actually pay them in the commission fee. So it might cost you money to *not* work with a professional agent!

Here's a quick story to illustrate what I mean:

I met a really nice couple, Nancy and Ryan. They wanted me

to do a market analysis on a house they had just purchased twelve months earlier, as they had decided to move to St. Paul. When my market analysis report came in ten thousand dollars under what they had paid a year ago, they were shocked.

I have NO idea how that financing went through, but it did.

The agent they had at the time said it was a steal and convinced them to write a full price offer "before someone else snapped it up."

I later found out that this agent had the listing for nearly six months and was about to lose it to another agent when her listing contract expired. Needless to say, she wanted to sell it quickly. Not very ethical, but that's what happened. And the kids believed her.

There was NO negotiating at all. None.

After trying for weeks to convince them that they needed to lower the price, they still wouldn't budge. Reluctantly, I let them list it for "their" price. Of course, there was no interest, no showings, and no offers. Two months later, they lost the house they had wanted in St. Paul because theirs didn't sell.

If you buy or sell a few homes over the course of your lifetime, it's not unrealistic to say that you could earn or lose one hundred thousand dollars based on how skilled of a negotiator you are. Think about how that will affect your retirement lifestyle, your children's college savings, or the amount you can donate to your church.

And the moral of the story is: Learn how to make money at the negotiating table!

PS: If your agent is knowledgeable, he or she will also tell you when you SHOULD write that full price offer, or even higher than full price. There *are* times that it's necessary. If a property truly is a high demand property (maybe in foreclosure, an estate sale, or other special circumstances) it could be priced to sell quickly.

As we've discussed, those properties *do* get multiple offers on them. You may be coached to offer more than the asking price. This can happen! Again, I can't stress enough the importance of having the right person giving you advice.

It's all about trust. You've *got* to *trust* your agent! If you don't, find a new agent.

6. Being Intimidated By the Numbers (And How to Make Over $100,000 in 20 Years or Less by Buying Instead of Renting)

Don't be blinded by numbers.

What I mean by that is: In addition to looking at the overall price tag, think about *affordable monthly payments*.

Remember: if you buy a house for one hundred and eighty thousand, you most likely won't be expected to write a check for that entire amount at closing. (Though if you are able and wish to do so, more power to you – you'll have great negotiating leverage based upon that!) But most people will end up making monthly payments. And since we either make monthly payments for rent or monthly payments for a mortgage, that number may be of greater importance than the actual price tag.

Can you afford the payments?

Are they better or worse (when taxes and insurance are added in, and utilities accounted for) than what you would otherwise spend in rent?

If so, don't let the *big number* intimidate you. And keep a formula handy as you shop, or your loan officer on speed-dial, in order to compare payments as you shop.

And really, this is a miracle from a historical perspective. Without our modern financial system that allows people to make affordable monthly payments, how many people would be homeowners? That's why many people define homeownership as **the American dream.**

I mean, think about it: even for a starter home priced at one-twenty, how long would it take you to save up the entire amount?

You could probably do it, but it would take years. *Decades*, most likely. Is it worth it to you to wait *decades* to invest in a home?

If you are thirty years old right now, you might be sixty before you finally have saved up enough money to buy a house. That's a pretty big price to pay.

Without getting too philosophical here, the one thing you cannot get more of is *time.* Everything else in life can be replaced: cars, clothes, jobs, computers, and so on. But even the richest man on

Earth cannot buy himself another year if he is dying. Time is not unlimited. It's a finite resource. It's the one thing you cannot buy more of.

You can't exchange dollars for more time... *or can you*?

When you agree to finance a home purchase by paying for it with a mortgage, you are essentially trading dollars for time.

You are agreeing to pay a little bit more in the form of *interest* for the privilege of owning a home NOW, instead of having to wait until you've saved up enough money to write a check for the entire amount.

For many folks, they will never have enough money saved up to buy a house. For example, if you are making twenty-five thousand per year, you will probably never be able to save up one hundred thousand to buy a house. After all of your living expenses are factored in, there simply won't be a lot of money left over every month. It would be extremely difficult, if not downright impossible, to buy a house without a mortgage.

That's why mortgages are so amazing! It allows the average

American to invest in homeownership by making monthly payments. Most people would agree that they'd rather pay some interest on their monthly payments to actually *own* a home, rather than renting for years and years and years.

Oh, and did I mention that when you rent, there is an *opportunity cost* to that money?

Let's say it takes you twenty years to save up one hundred grand to buy a house. This means that you're saving about five thousand dollars a year, or $416 per month. **After twenty years of saving $416 per month**, you finally have enough money in your savings account to go out and buy your hundred thousand dollar house.

But look at the *opportunity cost* of the situation: Instead of saving that $416 every month in a savings account (which pays little to no interest) how else could you have invested that money?

Imagine that when you started saving your $416 per month you were twenty-five years old. This means that you'd be forty-five by the time you're able to buy your house! And you won't be living in a high-end luxury home… in Minneapolis, one hundred thousand will buy you a dated starter home at best. (Good thing you have *vision*, because you're going to need it. Also good thing that you like North Minneapolis, because that's where you're going to end up with this price point.)

With a budget of one hundred grand, you won't have high-end appliances, newer flooring, an updated kitchen, modern bathrooms, a big yard, or similar.

Here's the **opportunity cost** of the situation: during the twenty years you were saving up $416 per month, you needed to live somewhere. You probably rented. Let's say you were spending five hundred a month on rent (in Minneapolis that would be a steal. I know people who charge more than that for one room in their house, to a roommate).

When you pay rent to the landlord, you are essentially paying their bills; their mortgage, their expenses.

<u>But you never see that money again.</u> It's not like when you move out you can ask for all the rent money you've paid. If you pay five hundred a month in rent, as soon as you mail that check, it's *gone*. Forever.

For the twenty years you've been saving up money to buy a house, **you will spend about ONE HUNDRED AND TWENTY THOUSAND DOLLARS on rent.**

Twenty years is two hundred and forty months.

240 months x $500/month = $120,000.

Yikes.

So if you think paying interest is so terrible that you're willing to wait twenty years to save up enough money to pay cash, are you prepared to live in your parents' basement that entire time? If not, be prepared to spend six figures or more on rent during this period.

What is the moral of the story? It makes sense to focus on the *monthly payment.* NOT the actual sales price.

Yes, you will pay more than the sticker price once interest is factored in. And yes, some financial gurus like Dave Ramsey think it's a terrible idea to pay interest on a home (for the record, I *love* Dave Ramsey and most of his advice is spot on).

But once you factor in the opportunity cost of paying all of that rent money, the decision is easy: go buy a house!

Whenever you hear someone say that homeownership is "too expensive," train yourself to ask the question, *expensive relative to what?*

ESPECIALLY in North Minneapolis, this is a no-brainer.

On the Northside, homes are still cheap enough that renting makes ZERO sense. I know that's a pretty bold statement, but think about it: if you have the financial discipline and responsibility necessary to own a home, why would you pay rent?

When you pay rent, it's basically a 100% interest payment. You are not paying any principal. You are not building any equity. Once that money is spent, it is gone.

This is not the case in all areas of the country. In some cities it makes financial sense to rent, because homes are so expensive (places like San Francisco or New York City). In that case, there would actually be an opportunity cost of *not* renting. This is NOT true in most parts of Minneapolis. Homes in many communities —especially Northside- are very, very affordable.

If you're paying five hundred a month in rent, why not invest *that same amount of money* every month in a mortgage payment? In a very literal sense, it wouldn't cost you a single penny to become a homeowner (there *are* programs out there to buy a home with zero down).

Sure, there will be costs associated with homeownership that don't exist for renters. Renters don't have to pay to re-shingle a roof every twenty-five years, upgrade aging furnaces, or repair plumbing. But renters *are* paying for these things, indirectly. The rent money they pay every month gives the homeowner the cash to make these improvements.

Wouldn't you rather be the one *receiving* money than sending it? When you pay your own monthly mortgage, you're basically *paying yourself.*

After interest is deducted, the money you pay every month pays down the balance of your mortgage.

Think about it: if you're renting for five hundred per year it equates to six thousand per year. Wouldn't you rather have that six thousand go into *your* property than the landlord's?

By buying instead of renting, you are spending the same amount of money—but instead of that cash going to the landlord it's being deposited into your home's equity "savings account."

Eventually, you'll pay the mortgage off entirely.

The one hundred twenty thousand you would have paid is now cash in your pocket—the money you would have spent on renting all those years.

Yes, there will be other expenses. Property taxes, home maintenance, and utilities, for example. But keep in mind that when you are renting, you are indirectly paying for all of these things anyway.

Now, you probably think I'm biased because I'm a real estate agent. That is true. I'm passionate about real estate! But you cannot ignore the simple math.

So if you're looking for a house and you put a certain dollar amount in your head as the maximum you are willing to spend, but you haven't considered it from the monthly-payment angle, you could be missing out on some great opportunities. Many buyers, even before checking with their loan officer, decide what they want to spend. They let *the big number* get in the way.

Why? **Because it intimidates them.** They get scared. They can't conceptualize paying that much money for something—it just *feels* like a big number.

For instance, they will think about a one hundred fifty thousand dollar house and only see that big dollar amount. To make matters worse, they will figure out how much interest they will pay on that amount, over the next thirty years.

It seems like a logical angle of approach, and thirty years seems a ridiculously long time.

Instead of stressing about the big number, focus on the affordable monthly payments. Are you comfortable with *that* number? If so, buy the house.

With today's interest rates being incredibly low (which could change by the time you're reading this book), you would be surprised at how low the payments really are.

Let's say you've decided that you don't want to spend one

dime more than one hundred fifty thousand. But a house comes along that's listed at one sixty-nine five. It is absolutely *perfect*. It's your dream home. Your real estate agent tells you that you can probably get it for one-sixty. *But that's TEN THOUSAND over your limit.* You don't have an extra ten grand laying around!

Instead of looking at the sales price, focus on the monthly payment. Especially when interest rates are reasonable, the difference in monthly payment between a one-fifty and one-sixty mortgage is about fifty bucks a month.

Can you handle an extra fifty dollars per month to live in your dream home? For most of us, the answer is YES!

Don't let a fear of big numbers intimidate you. Focus on a monthly payment that you can comfortably afford.

7. Having Unrealistic Expectations

David and Emily wanted to look at homes in a certain area (ahem, South Minneapolis excluding Central, Powderhorn and Phillips) and were on a tight budget. Keep in mind it was their very first home, so they weren't spending two-fifty. Well, they weren't spending even *close* to that.

In fact, they weren't even spending *half* of that.

But they were used to spacious, luxurious homes (belonging to their parents and friends) and had developed some unrealistic expectations. They were assuming they could buy two hundred thousand dollars' worth of house for a little over one hundred. I knew from the start this would be an interesting house hunting process.

David and Emily needed a reality check. I tried to explain this to them at our initial meeting over coffee at Victory 44. They didn't really listen to me when I tried to tell them that their wish list of "must haves" was completely unrealistic for their budget.

And I mean <u>completely</u> unrealistic.

They wanted four bedrooms, hardwood floors, an updated kitchen, a modern master bath suite, and yard "suitable for entertaining."

I had to muster all of my professional courtesy to not to spit out my coffee when they handed me their list of "must haves." I actually thought for a moment that I might be the victim of a reality

TV show prank. It would be hard to find a home that satisfied their list even with a budget of fifty percent higher!

That first meeting at Victory 44 (strategically planned on my part to expose them to the Victory neighborhood, I admit) didn't go very smoothly. They claimed to understand my concerns, but tried to convince me that if I looked hard enough, I would find the perfect home for them.

Sorry, I am a Realtor, not a miracle worker, I thought to myself glumly. *I can help you find a "stretch" home that might be a little bit out of your price range and maybe convince the seller to bring it down to a price you can afford, but I can't magically double your budget.*

I'm not the federal government. I can't print money!

Anyway, I think we looked at twenty homes. They were absolutely *determined* to live in the same area as some of their friends (ahem, Longfellow/Nokomis) but honestly, we couldn't find anything in their price range that even came close to *remotely* satisfying their wish list.

The homes that *were* in their price range needed extensive

repairs—repairs that would require money David and Emily did not have.

I FINALLY convinced them to come back to Victory 44 for a latte and a re-grouping session. I told them to come via Theodore Wirth Parkway this time. And before our meeting, I asked them the following question:

If I were to find some homes that met all of your criteria, but weren't located in Longfellow or Nokomis, would you at least like me to send you the online listing information? Just to have a peek?

They agreed, and I sent them links to a couple of Tudors in Cleveland and Victory.

Can you guess what happened?

They ended up purchasing a beautiful home, close to the parkway, at a price well within their budget……**that was nicer than what any of their friends had.**

It's important to keep an open mind.

This is more important than ever when you're buying your first home. I get this a lot with young people in their twenties. Even the college dorms today are pretty nice, so many of these first time homebuyers have a completely unrealistic expectation of what a "starter home" is all about.

If you are twenty-something years old and reading this, pay attention!

The entire concept of a starter home is pretty simple: it's a home for you to *start* your home ownership experience. It won't be luxurious. It probably won't be spacious. It won't have a newly updated kitchen or a beautiful bathroom like you see in the home and decorating magazines. A starter home is usually small (two or three bedrooms), and has one bathroom. Sometimes two.

A starter home will allow you to build a solid credit history, because the monthly payments will be affordable.

As I've mentioned elsewhere in this book, this is NOT TRUE IN OTHER AREAS OF THE COUNTRY. In fact, usually when I go out of the area (or out of state) to industry conferences, my colleagues are often shocked when I tell them how affordable homes are in my market.

The usual reply I get is, "Why would ANYONE rent? If homes

are that cheap, everyone should buy!"

All I can do is nod my head in agreement.

And truth be told, it's a great feeling knowing that you have money left over every month. Many people make the mistake of buying at the absolute top of what they can afford, so there isn't much left at the end of every month for things like entertainment, vacations, and emergencies. This can be a stressful spot to put yourself in.

It's better to buy an affordable starter home that's well within your budget, and have plenty of breathing room every month. You'll be a happier person, I guarantee it. As your career develops and you start earning more money, *then* you can look into buying a nicer home with a larger mortgage payment.

I do NOT recommend buy a *reach* home (where you're reaching a bit beyond what you can actually afford) as your first home. This could be a HUGE mistake.

Remember: a starter home is all about building a solid financial foundation.

A starter home will not *only* help you build a solid credit history. It's a great learning experience! Owning a home gives you an entirely new perspective on "living." When you own the house you live in, you will notice things you didn't notice before.

- The condition of the siding.
- The condition of the shingles on the roof.
- The efficiency of your mechanical systems.

I could probably rattle off a dozen more, but here's what I'm getting at: home owners have to be responsible for many things that tenants take for granted. This awareness gives you a new perspective on the true cost of having a brand new kitchen, updated bathroom, new flooring, and so on.

Homeownership is a crash course in the value of a hard earned dollar.

Tenants will often complain that a kitchen is ugly, a bathroom needs to be updated, or carpets need replacing. When you become a homeowner, and you begin to learn the cost of such things, it may start to make sense to you why most landlords don't spend gobs of money updating their properties—it often doesn't make financial sense.

A modest kitchen renovation could set you back ten grand. Updating a bathroom can easily cost a few thousand dollars. New flooring adds up quickly, too. For a landlord to justify investing this much money back into a house, he or she would need to charge a lot more in rent, which *very few* renters are interested in paying.

Once you own your own home, all of these things start to make sense.

With any luck, your home will appreciate while you own it. So not only will you build up equity by paying down the mortgage every month, you will increase your net worth through appreciation of your home's value. (There are also ways to "force" appreciation that I cover elsewhere in the book.)

In summary, investing in a starter home is a very, very valuable thing to do. It will allow you to build your credit, become a more responsible person, and financially position you to invest in your dream home someday.

A journey of a thousand miles begins with a single step, so

don't let unrealistic expectations stop you from buying your first starter home!

8. Not Conducting a PROFESSIONAL Home Inspection

When I first started buying and selling investment property, home inspections weren't as common as they are today. Sometimes a buyer would have a trusted friend take a look at the house, possibly an electrician, plumber, or someone they knew with construction experience. It wasn't anything formal, and it didn't really affect the buying process one way or another.

Professional investors were much more likely to do their due diligence on a property, because they performed more organized calculations of the costs associated with things like deferred maintenance and future renovation expenses.

But for the average residential homebuyer, it was not uncommon to trust that the seller wasn't hiding any problems. And for many homes, that was quite a leap of faith.

Today, it's become standard to have a professional home inspection before closing on a house.

If you don't already know, a home inspection involves a home inspector going through everything in the house and making sure that any obvious problems are identified in advance of closing. Home inspectors will generally check the roof to see the condition of the shingles, they will check the siding, they will examine the walls and ceilings for signs of water leaks, they will check all sinks and faucets, they will check the power outlets, they will check the age and condition of the HVAC system components, and more. Depending on who you hire, it can range from basic to exhaustive.

On an average size house, a home inspection will take approximately two hours.

As of the writing of this book, home inspections average between three and four hundred dollars to conduct. As I've said elsewhere in the book, this is ALWAYS negotiable.

The cost of a home inspection is almost always paid by the buyer at the time of the inspection.

Trust me on this one—it will be the best four hundred dollars you ever spend. I've had instances where a problem was discovered during the routine home inspection that potentially saved the buyer over ten thousand dollars. That's a pretty good return on investment!

<u>Personally, I wouldn't even CONSIDER buying a home without an inspection.</u>

You can breathe a sigh of relief once the home inspection report has been transmitted. The only thing a home inspector *can't* do is rip open the walls to see what's inside, or start tearing open the flooring. Other than that, the home inspection should reveal any potential problems, fixes, and repairs that need to be made before closing.

Following a home inspection, it's not uncommon for a buyer to request that the seller make repairs of issues discovered during that inspection.

<u>But let me be very, very, very clear on this:</u> the home inspection is not meant to create a laundry list of repairs for the seller. Unless you're moving into a brand new home, there *will be* maintenance issues. It's just a fact of life.

A good home inspector will coach you through all of this, and teach you how to be proactive when it comes to *preventative maintenance*. Your car regularly needs oil changes and tire rotations, right? Well your house is no different. If you fell in love with a great used car, you wouldn't *not* buy it because it's in need of an oil change. The same goes for purchasing a house. Don't let minor, correctable problems get between you and your dream home.

If the extent of the repairs is over a few hundred dollars, you may need to renegotiate the price if the seller isn't willing to make those repairs. Again, consult with your real estate agent and home inspector. It's ultimately up to you, but they will be able to provide you with the wisdom necessary to make the right decision.

And remember: everything is negotiable.

I almost *always* advise my buyer clients to include an inspection addendum in their offer, **making that offer contingent upon satisfactory results of a home inspection.**

This allows you to walk away from a sale even *after* you've made an official legal offer, if the inspection reveals the home isn't up to your standards.

And the beauty of this clause is that your standards are legally subjective. What this means is that you can say the house "failed" the inspection *for any reason.* You can literally point to ANYTHING in the home inspection report and use it as an escape clause from a potentially bad deal.

And assuming the seller accepts your offer with the contingency included, this is completely ethical.

There is nothing wrong with using the home inspection clause to exit a deal. If the home inspector finds something that you feel is a deal breaker, *then it's a deal breaker!* This can be anything from a leak under the bathroom sink to a few missing shingles.

But, keep in mind, if you truly want the house, you won't allow a few minor repairs to stop you from buying the house.

In fact, I would venture to say that it's nearly impossible for a home inspection to *not* reveal things that need to be repaired.

It is almost guaranteed that the home inspector will discover problems with the home. When you hire a home inspector, you should EXPECT there to be problems detailed in the report. Usually, these problems are not a big deal.

AND THIS IS WHERE MANY HOMEBUYERS FREAK OUT.

Pay close attention here: because of potential liability, a home inspector can be inclined to make things sound worse than they probably are.

Consequently, some homebuyers freak out when they receive the home inspection: *"Oh my God! There are four missing shingles, the kitchen sink leaks, and one of the window needs to be replaced!"*

At this point, you need to *slow down*.

Try to evaluate the situation logically and not emotionally. Replacing a few shingles, fixing a basic leak, and replacing a window is *not that big of a deal.*

In fact, most everything short of finding dead bodies hidden in the basement can be fixed.

Do NOT let the home inspection intimidate you or scare you. Know that the home inspection report will make it sound much worse than it actually is (the home inspector doesn't want to get sued, so he will write down every single defect he can possibly find).

Don't let a few imperfections scare you away. You will end up spending money on maintenance anyway, so it's better to proactively find out than *react* to a problem that has compounded over time.

Your real estate agent can also help you identify issues on your initial showing, but don't rely on them to substitute for an inspector's expertise. Real estate agents (usually) are not qualified home inspectors.

This subject reminds me of the first property I ever purchased. The year was 1999, and I was twenty-one years old. I didn't have much money, but I had a lot of vision. So much vision, in fact, that I think it scared my Realtor a bit. We looked at a lot of dumps!

Since I only had forty thousand dollars (yes you read that number correctly) to spend, my options were <u>severely</u> limited. But we found a house that I fell in love with, and made a bid on. It was a duplex in the Phillips neighborhood, built in the 1880s. It was boarded and winterized, and the open attic window apertures provided something of a boarding house for the neighborhood pigeon population. But oh, how I swooned over the woodwork and high ceilings.

I made an offer the same day I saw the property, and did not inspect. And I got the house! I was elated.

After closing, I called the city to have someone come out and turn the water on at the stop box in the street, which had been turned off for I-don't-know-how-long. The city worker was very nice, and I think he might have taken a bit of pity on me, as he undoubtedly saw right away that I had no idea what I was doing. He walked me through the house beforehand, instructing me to open all the faucets so that water could flow through and fill the system in an orderly fashion. I did that, and then we went out to turn things on at the street.

When I walked back into the house, I heard running water, and thought: *success!* But then I went back to the first floor bathroom, and saw that the water I had heard was not only coming from the faucet (at a trickle) but indeed also running down all four walls!

What a disaster. I had no idea that the pipes had long ago frozen and burst.

I bet an inspector might have thought to look for that ahead of time, since it's a fairly common issue with vacant homes in our climate. And I should add that I might well have still bought the house even if an inspector alerted me to the issue in advance. The house was very cheap relative to the character and other good qualities, and I ended up living there quite happily for four years. But if I had known in advance about the plumbing issue, I could have prepared myself, both financially and psychologically.

Instead, I learned the hard way. The VERY hard way. Hopefully others can learn from my mistake and not have to go through something similar.

Here's what you need to remember: always, always, always have a home inspection before buying a house. But at the same time, don't let the home inspection report scare you away from investing in the home of your dreams. All houses have some issues, and the majority of them are fixable.

PS: I bought the house in the middle of winter. When spring rains came, I learned that the roof leaked. And with the first blustery storm of summer, half my chimney fell off into the yard. I'm still glad I bought that house. But oh, what a harsh teacher it was.

9. Letting Friends, Family, and Other Non-Experts Influence *YOUR* Decision

We'll keep this section short and sweet.

Try not to allow unsolicited opinions from friends, family, or other non-experts to have too much influence on your home buying decision.

The exception would obviously be if you have friends or family that work professionally in the real estate or construction industries.

I've heard this too many times to count:

Constance, our parents need to look with us!

If your parents will be living in the new house with you, that makes complete sense.

If not, I suggest that you do some independent research on what *you* want, go house hunting, find your top three houses, and THEN bring your family in to look, after you've already toured the properties yourself.

Our parents all have wisdom and experience which we, their children, do not, and I completely understand the desire to make use of that in the home-buying process. After all, they've probably bought and sold a home or two, and they may be able to provide some long-term perspective. But beware of abdicating all responsibility and decision making to them.

I see scenarios like this often: a young couple falls in love with a home. It's in their budget and it's in a neighborhood they like. But the parents object to it for some reason. Not wanting to insult their parents, the buyers walk away from a sale. After all, they don't want to ask for their parents' advice and then ignore it.

But keep in mind that most peoples' *parents are not real estate experts.*

If there is something inherently wrong with a sale, the real estate agent should advise you accordingly. If you like a home, the real estate agent thinks it's a good fit, and the bank agrees to finance the mortgage, do it! At that point, any other opinions are exactly that—*opinions.*

I mean, you wouldn't let your parents perform brain surgery

on you just because they are your parents. The same goes for your friends, coworkers, or anyone else that feels the need to tell you what you should or shouldn't buy.

Politely thank them for their suggestions, and then do whatever you were going to do.

I am not trying to be disrespectful to parents. I am one. But you should know that the vast majority of real estate agents cringe when they learn that their first-time homebuyers want to bring the parents to showings. Because a good many parents are overprotective and don't want their children buying a house with so much as hairline crack in a plaster wall.

This is where it's most important to find an agent you TRUST.

And as a parent, if you see the top three homes your child selected and think they are all terrible, talk to the agent! Part of the problem may be price range. Don't worry if your son or daughter can't afford their dream home at age twenty-five.

It's far better for them to build a solid credit history, learn the ropes of homeownership, and become a financially responsible young adult than it is to buy a *stretch* home at the top of their budget that leaves them broke at the end of every month because of an expensive mortgage payment.

The other issue I sometimes see with well-intentioned parents is comparing the current market to what it was when *they* purchased.

I can't tell you how many times I have heard, *"Well when we bought our house in 1970, it was only forty thousand and it was twice this size!"*

Ummmmm… inflation. Most everything was cheaper in 1970. That doesn't mean your son or daughter is getting ripped off buying their home. If it's priced well *relative to the market right now*, that's all you need to worry about.

Advice is good, but *don't make unrealistic comparisons.* You will be frustrated, and so will everyone else.

10. Expecting it to be Like *HGTV*

In the next few pages, I'm going to reveal a secret about how hit TV shows like *House Hunters* are set up behind the scenes.

You didn't *actually* think it was real, did you?

But first, some honest advice about house hunting.

The home buying process doesn't always go smoothly. And especially if it's your first time buying a home, the process can be downright intimidating.

There are lots of forms to sign. Lots of paperwork. Lots of meetings. You will have to put your money where your mouth is at offer-writing time in the form of an earnest money check, to show that you are serious.

It will seem like the bank wants all sorts of things from you: recent paycheck stubs, last year's taxes, a credit report, and more.

You WILL get stressed out. Accept this as a fact before you get started.

All sorts of things will be running through your mind.

Title insurance… wait, what's a title? And what am I insuring?

Speaking of insurance, I need to insure my home! Where do I go for that? Does it cover fire damage? Hail? What if we have a water leak? And how much does it cost?

Cost...yikes. I wonder what utilities will cost every month. Will someone send me a bill? Or do I have to go somewhere to pay it?

And how do I pay the mortgage every month? Can I set that up on auto-pay?

And closing costs... how much will those be? And what exactly am I paying for?

Here's my advice to you: accept the fact that at some point, you WILL be overwhelmed. You WILL be stressed out. You WILL be confused. You might be afraid to ask a "dumb question." You might start to experience doubts. You might question whether or not buying a home was such a good idea.

<u>This is completely normal. *Everyone* experiences this</u>.

But it's much easier to navigate the home buying process when you are mentally prepared.

If you acknowledge ahead of time that there will be things you don't understand, you won't let it dominate your thoughts.

Real life is not like HGTV.

Reality TV is staged.

With the popular show *House Hunters*, the couple has already purchased the home they end up "selecting" in the end. (Sorry if I just ruined the fun for you.)

On shows like *House Hunters*, they are basically pretending the entire time that they are looking at homes. In reality, they've already chosen the home they are going to live in. They've already bought it.

House hunting is more complex than the thirty minutes of edited footage you see on TV.

There might be bumps in the road. Actually, let me rephrase that. There WILL BE BUMPS IN THE ROAD. In fact, there might be some twelve-inch potholes deep enough to get lost in.

Whether it's a home inspection issue, a financing issue, or just not finding what you're looking for, try to be *patient*. Remember your goal.

You don't want to be a renter any longer. You want to be a home OWNER. The financial security that comes with owning your own home, and the *feeling* of owning your home, will make everything worth it. Trust me.

11. Not Signing a Contract with a Buyer's Agent

I think I may have mentioned this already, but it bears repeating:

Do not simply call the phone number on the yard sign.

Why? The phone number on the yard sign is the *listing* agent's phone number. The listing agent is contractually obligated to represent the best interests of the *seller*. Not yours.

This means that they won't really give you objective information, advice, or insights on the property. They have one obligation, legally and ethically, and that is to sell the house for the price and terms that are most beneficial to the seller.

The listing agent doesn't need to be concerned about whether the home is right for you, or if the price makes sense for you.

They. Represent. The. Seller.

I mean, think about it: as a buyer, does it make any sense, whatsoever, to work with someone who is legally obligated to do what's best for the other side?

Instead, find an agent you trust. Find an agent you are comfortable with. And then sign an exclusive contract to work with them.

What signing a contract does is insure that your agent is obligated to do what is best for *you*. They will research homes for *you*. They will submit offers for *you*. They will negotiate for *you*. They will do what's in your best interest, not the seller's. This is a huge advantage.

And the best part? The buyer's agent only gets paid when you actually buy a house (usually their commission is paid *by the seller*).

So you can rest assured that you are getting objective information from your buyer agent. They have no incentive to lie, mislead, deceive, or try to convince you to buy a home that's not right for you.

YOU are their client. Not the seller. They want to do what's right for *you*. If they don't, they won't get paid.

Unfortunately, it's very common for new buyers to start by

poking around online, followed by driving around to see the outside of interesting homes, and then end up calling a number on a sign. Some will talk with five different agents in a month!

Guess what? <u>Most agents really aren't interested in working with you if you aren't loyal to them.</u> This isn't because they feel entitled - it's just not a good use of their time to spend hours and hours with someone that might end up buying a home with another agent. It would be like a car salesperson spending lots of time with a customer, taking them on multiple test drives, helping them understand the financing, only to have the customer buy that vehicle through the salesperson from one cubicle over.

Clearly, real estate agents don't want to invest a bunch of time and money into a client that views the various agents as interchangeable commodities.

When you sign a buyer agreement contract to work exclusively with one agent, that agent is now incentivized to work for *you*. They will have *your* best interests in mind.

And remember: they don't get paid until you actually buy a new home.

There simply is no reason to purchase real estate without your own exclusive buyer representation.

Of course, it's important to make sure you choose the agent that's right for you. There are many different Realtors out there, with different styles and areas of expertise. Pick the one that fits best with your style and needs. It will take a lot of the stress out of your home buying process.

12. Giving Up Too Easily

Where there's a will, there's a way.

Because the average person is not buying or selling multiple homes every single month, they often don't realize how flexible terms can actually be. I see it happen far too often where "conventional" financing won't work, and a buyer gets discouraged and quits. Sometimes they feel embarrassed that their credit score isn't perfect. They feel shame in not being able to qualify for a traditional mortgage with a bank, so they simply give up.

This might be a big mistake.

They often get discouraged, and embarrassment prevents

them from exploring creative options. Buyers don't want to be perceived as *desperate*, and they certainly don't want to experience "failure" again.

It's important to understand though, that many people don't qualify for traditional financing.

Maybe their credit score isn't good enough, they don't have enough money saved up for a down payment, their expenses are too high, or their income is too low. Or maybe they are self-employed and don't have two years of solid tax returns to show.

Maybe you have enough money to make the monthly payment, but your *ratios* aren't up to the bank's standards. For example, banks usually don't want you to be spending more than thirty percent of your monthly income on a mortgage. So, hypothetically, if you're earning one thousand dollars per month, the bank won't lend you money to buy a home if the monthly mortgage will exceed three hundred dollars, which is thirty percent of your income. There are other metrics the bank will look at, but the point I'm trying to make is that often times you actually do have the money to make the payment every month, but you're not as financially stable as the bank would like you to be. The bank doesn't want to risk having you get behind on your payments or going into default, so they refuse to make the loan in the first place.

Things weren't always like this. When the housing boom was in in full swing a few years ago, many banks weren't even doing basic credit or income verification. Anyone, and I mean anyone, qualified to buy a house. Even with nothing down! It was crazy. This was because the local banks would "originate" the loan, then larger government-backed institutions would buy the mortgage from the local bank. At that point, the local bank that created the loan didn't have any risk. The mortgage wasn't on their books. If the homeowner defaulted, it wasn't their problem. This obviously created a conflict of interest, because the people profiting off of loan origination didn't really have any incentive to do basic qualification of their borrowers' ability to pay.

If you were a buyer, this was great! You didn't need to worry about qualifying for a mortgage. *Everyone* qualified. Today, this is not the case. And it's why I'm writing this chapter, to reveal some lesser-known alternatives to financing your home purchase.

Once again, where there's a will, there's a way. Creative financing techniques might be an option, if the buyer is motivated AND the seller is motivated.

In fact, if the <u>seller</u> is motivated, pretty much anything is possible. Sometimes the seller just needs to get rid of a house, and they will do anything necessary to make the sale work. As a buyer, this is a perfect situation to be in.

Maybe they owe money for something else, and the only way they can come up with the cash is selling the house.

Maybe it's an estate sale, and the family just wants to sell the property and not have to worry about maintenance and taxes.

Maybe the seller is moving out of state for a new job, and needs to sell quickly.

Maybe the seller is a landlord, and is sick of managing tenants.

Whatever the motivation, the first step in creative financing is working with a motivated seller. If the seller isn't motivated, none of the creative strategies I will teach you will work—the home will most likely be purchased by another buyer who *is* qualified for normal financing.

From the seller's perspective, it's easier to work with a buyer who's prequalified for a mortgage. They get a lump sum check from the bank, and that's that. It's far more convenient for the bank to finance a property.

But, like I said, if a seller is desperate--and they're running out of options--they *will* be open to more creative alternatives.

<u>The first step is making sure the seller is motivated.</u>

If the seller is motivated, nine times out of ten the most common financing strategy involves some form of *seller financing*. This means that instead of using a bank as the middleman, the buyer will make payments directly to the seller. Sometimes this takes the form of a *contract for deed*. Instead of paying the bank a monthly mortgage payment, you pay the money directly to the seller. There is no bank involved.

Typically, the seller will charge a premium to compensate for the risk and inconvenience of not using a bank. Usually homes sold on a contract for deed will include an interest rate that is slightly higher than a traditional mortgage. So if a conventional mortgage is 6%, the seller may demand 8%. The specific numbers will vary depending on the market.

Sometimes the seller will permit a small down payment, sometimes not. Often the down payment will be less than the traditional twenty percent down that a conventional loan would require. Sometimes the seller will request five percent down, or ten percent down. But not always—if the seller is motivated, you *can* find properties for zero down. I'm not saying you *should* do this, but it is possible.

Where there's a will, there's a way.

Sometimes a seller isn't willing to finance the property forever, but they will for a year or two. They are hoping you will qualify for a traditional mortgage in that time frame.

Sometimes the seller will be open to bartering for services. If you're an auto mechanic, perhaps you can trade services as a bargaining piece. Would the seller value free oil changes for five years, along with free car maintenance? The only way to find out is to ask.

The worst that can happen is they say no.

Creative financing options aren't for everyone, though. Sometimes it can be a really bad idea. Other times it's exactly what is needed to make a sale happen that otherwise wouldn't.

And this is yet another reason why it's so important to work with a real estate agent that you *trust*. A good real estate agent can guide you through this process and make sure you are aware of the various options. They will make sure you understand the risks, the pros and cons, and what is ultimately best for *you*.

Every situation is different.

If you really want a specific house, and the seller is motivated to sell it, your creativity *can* be a wonderful substitute for money. Just because a bank won't loan you money doesn't mean someone else won't. Don't give up!

13. Buying Too Much House

Elsewhere in this book, I try to convince you that often you *can* afford more than you think you can.

This is because it pains me to see buyers say no to a home that they love when it's only slightly over an *arbitrary* budget. When it's amortized over a thirty-year mortgage, the difference in monthly payment just isn't that much money.

However, the opposite is also true. And probably worse.

Buying a home that is too expensive for your budget virtually *guarantees* you won't be happy. Even if you love the home.

Think about it: is it better to err on the side of buying a home that's a bit more plain that what you hoped for (and having extra money left over each month), or buying a home that's out of your price range and having to constantly worry about paying the mortgage?

A monthly mortgage payment is exactly that: it's a **monthly** payment.

If you struggle to make the payment in April, it's going to be just as hard to make the payment in May. And June. And July. And so on, for the next thirty years.

Unless your finances change for the better (you get

promoted, get a higher paying job elsewhere, inherit money or work weekends on a hobby business) a monthly payment that stretches your budget will continue to stretch your budget.

Is it worth it?

I'm not even going to pretend that the answer to this question is subjective. It's not a matter of opinion. It is simply not worth it.

If you don't have a specific plan that details how you will pay for a home that is out of your price range, then you have no business even *looking* at these homes.

Every dollar you pay in a mortgage payment is a dollar you cannot invest for profit somewhere else.

At best, the equity in your home resembles a savings account. It's really not an investment in the same way a mutual fund, stock, or bond is.

I'm not saying real estate is a bad investment—I'm saying *the home you personally live in* should not be viewed as an investment.

Even worse, it should not be your *only* investment.

Your home is not a magical ATM. Do not assume it will constantly increase in value, allowing you to borrow against it with home equity loans.

Don't put all your eggs in one basket.

For many Americans, their home is their only investment. They have no money invested in stocks, bonds, mutual funds, certificates of deposit, land, rental real estate, actual businesses, precious metals, or other investment vehicles. If your home equity reflects your net worth, you're in trouble if the local housing market dips—even temporarily.

If your home appreciates in value and your equity increases, then great. Think of that as a bonus. It's icing on the cake. Don't attempt to rationalize a mortgage payment you can't afford by convincing yourself that the home is an investment.

That mentality got *a lot* of people in trouble a few years ago.

Patience IS a virtue. Step back, take a reality check, and buy with your pocket book, not with your heart.

If you buy a home with a mortgage payment so high that you

don't have any money left over every month for savings, investment accounts, vacation fund, emergency fund or entertainment money, you will be miserable.

Let me repeat that: **you will be miserable.** Regardless of how nice your house is.

It's simply no fun to have to turn down your friends when they ask you if you want to go shopping next weekend, go out to eat, or go to a Twins game.

Do you *really* want that extra bedroom, or high-end updated kitchen, if it means you'll only have twenty dollars per month of disposable entertainment income? Or zero?

I mean, seriously - who cares if you have a nice home in a nice neighborhood if you can't enjoy life?

There is a difference between buying a *reach* house that is slightly out of your price range (with a specific plan on how you will pay for it), and buying a home that you simply cannot afford *with no plan whatsoever on how you'll come up with the money every single month.*

And let me repeat that for emphasis: every single month.

In fact, some months it will actually be worse than others.

For those of us living in Minnesota, our housing expenses fluctuate with the seasons. Your utility bills can be *much* more expensive in the winter due to heating costs that simply don't exist in the summer.

If you are stretched so thin that you're worried about making the monthly payments, things will only get worse come winter time. Factor that in when you're putting together budgets and figuring out how much house you can buy.

It is not worth it to have a monthly mortgage payment looming over your head every month that you can't afford.

It is stressful.

You will *not* enjoy living in a larger, newer home if you never have extra money to buy new clothes, go shopping, go out to eat, or take vacations. You will end up focusing on what you can't have instead of what you do have. And that's no way to live.

It is much wiser to invest in a home you can comfortably

afford, and have extra money left over each paycheck to have fun with. And that's assuming you're financially responsible and have already allocated some money to retirement savings, the kids' college fund, and your emergency reserves.

Don't worry—as your career develops, you *will* earn more money and someday be in the financial position to buy the dream house you've always wanted.

If you've got your eye on a half a million dollar riverfront townhome, it can happen! With diligent saving, a successful career, and responsible financial decisions, of course. Just don't buy a five hundred thousand dollar home when you're making fifty thousand per year.

If buying a home requires clever rationalization on your part, it's better to use that mental energy to earn more income and make smarter investments so that someday you *can* buy that riverfront property, and not think twice about the price tag.

Don't let your emotions get the best of you—you will be happier with a home you can afford.

14. Not Getting Pre-Qualified For a Mortgage

I can't think of a single good reason why you would NOT want to be prequalified for a mortgage. It makes the house hunting process so much easier.

In one of my ads promoting this book, I stated that after reading the book, you would know *the number one mistake made by homebuyers*.

Well, this is it.

The number one mistake made by homebuyers is NOT getting pre-qualified for a mortgage.

When you get pre-qualified, everything else falls into place. You know exactly how much you can spend, so you don't waste time looking at homes you can't afford, either online or in person. This will reduce stress for you *and* your real estate agent.

Getting pre-qualified is THE most important step to house hunting.

There is little that is more disheartening than to fall in love with a house, only to find out that you can't afford it. It's even more humiliating when you place an offer contingent on financing, and the financing falls through.

To get pre-qualified, the first step is finding a loan officer that you can trust.

Just like finding the right real estate agent, finding the right loan officer is critical. They are not all the same. It is well worth your time to shop around and figure out which loan officer best fits your personality and needs.

Sometimes you will really like your bank, but you don't click with the loan officer there. Sometimes the opposite happens—you don't really like a particular bank, but you enjoy working with a loan officer that works there. My advice would be to go with whatever loan officer you are most comfortable with.

It's more accurate to say that you are working with the specific, individual loan officer than you are working with the overall banking entity.

It should be someone you can actually look at face to face—beware of online financing! There are many big name companies out there like *Quicken Loans* that are probably reputable and trustworthy, but there are many scams out there as well.

They are not ALL bad, but why risk it?

I can virtually guarantee that you will be much happier (and less stressed) if you work with a local bank that has a *physical presence* in your community.

There's just something to be said about good old fashioned face-to-face conversation!

Unlike books, movie tickets, or other items commonly purchased online, a mortgage is difficult to process in the virtual world. It's simply too complex and personal of a process to be handled well online.

Maybe that will change in the coming years—I'm sure people were originally skeptical about many things that are sold online today. But for now, I advise my clients to avoid online mortgages.

It's simply too risky.

I have seen transactions fall apart the day of closing. I have also seen "good deals" be everything BUT good. They have a way of sneaking in some last minute surprise closing costs. This is how they remain profitable even though their advertised mortgage rates *seem* like really good deals (usually better than the rates at local banks).

For example, instead of the sixty-five hundred you were "quoted," you get to the closing table and find out they have some extra fees tacked on, and your closing costs are really closer to eight thousand dollars!

It's usually a much better idea to "keep it local," and work with a local lender that is truly part of the community.

Local lenders have accountability and incentive to serve you and get the deal done in a timely manner—it's much easier to complain about bad service when it's a local company than it is with an unknown online company.

Local banks can't afford to have negative word of mouth circulate in a community, so they are usually dedicated to providing great service!

You get what you pay for.

CHAPTER NINE

ARE YOU A FIRST-TIME HOMEBUYER?

SIX THINGS YOU MUST DO

Buying your first house can be scary.

It's a huge investment – quite possibly the biggest one you will ever make in your lifetime. And unless you grew up with parents who were real estate agents, you are probably a little intimidated by the whole process. Some common concerns include:

How do you know if you are buying the right house?

Who do you trust?

What do you need to know about your credit score?

When should you get pre-approved?

How much can you afford?

These are the kinds of questions that are probably racing through your mind right now. Hopefully this chapter will help you sort out some of the components, and contribute to making your first experience more pleasant and memorable.

And keep this in mind throughout the process: *it will be worth it to be a homeowner!*

1. Check Your Credit Score

Let's start from the top. In order to buy a home you're going to need to have at least *pretty good* credit. It doesn't have to be perfect, but it can't be below average or mediocre. So, now is the time to clean it up before you start the home buying process.

What you *don't* want are a bunch of surprises showing up on your score down the road when you are ready to close on a house. This is a *bad* time to find out that your credit isn't what you thought it was. I've had homebuyers cry on my shoulder (literally) when they found out their credit score prevented them from buying a home.

It's better to take care of this right away so you don't have to worry about it when you actually start house hunting—even if you are absolutely certain your score is good. You never know what could be on it.

You can get a copy of your credit score from the three major credit agencies, or by talking to a local bank:

- Experian
- Equifax
- TransUnion

2. Evaluate Your Credit Cards

When it comes to credit cards, you need to think wisely about how you are using them. Many, many, many young people abuse their plastic. Having bad habits with credit cards WILL prevent you from someday buying your first house. That's a fact.

This specifically haunts first time homebuyers, because they usually have a relatively low income. Because their expenses take up a larger chunk of that income, any additional credit card debt makes it difficult for a bank to justify loaning them money. They have a thin margin every month, and that is a concern for potential lenders.

Typically, banks don't want you to spend any more than thirty percent of your monthly income directly on housing. For example, if you're making two thousand a month, that equates to six hundred dollars. When you add credit card debt (which usually has very high interest rates) to the equation, banks will *not* approve your mortgage.

I'm not saying you can't have *some* credit card debt—it completely depends on your various income to expenses and debt ratios. *Preferably you have zero debt, and you pay your credit card balance in full every single month.* But remember: the worst type of debt to have is high interest rate credit card debt.

There *are* amazing "first time homebuyer" mortgage programs out there, but you need to have solid finances!

So before you even start *looking* at homes, get strategic about this. Read a Dave Ramsey book or two, and apply his advice. If you have outstanding credit card balances, pay them down to zero! Live frugally if you need to, and make temporary lifestyle sacrifices.

Trust me—it will feel amazing when you have little to no credit card debt, and you're able to qualify for a home because of your above average credit score.

3. Create a Budget

Before you ever buy a house you should create a monthly budget based upon what you would pay *if you already owned a house.*

This exercise has a number of advantages. First, it teaches you to live within your housing budget when it isn't as risky to do so. Living for three or four months on a "restricted" budget will give you an idea of whether or not your expectations are realistic.

In other words, it will teach you what you can truly afford. Better to find out when you have the income than when you already have the house…..but don't have the money.

In my experience, many first time homebuyers buy a house that's at the top of their budget. They technically can afford it, but they have little to no money left over every month for entertainment and extras. It's no fun to live in your own home if you can't go to the movies once a month, eat out with your friends, or take a basic vacation.

Plan accordingly.

In addition, you'll be able to save more money toward a potential down payment (which you should have been building for a number of years by now), pay off any remaining debt (like credit cards or car loans), save money for any moving expenses, and build an emergency fund.

And if you don't already have a few thousand dollars in an emergency fund, you really shouldn't buy a house. Things *will* go wrong. A furnace could go out (not a fun thing during Minnesota winters), air conditioning could stop working, water leaks in the ceiling, siding repaired, or your car could break down.

You NEED to have some liquid cash available to pay for unforeseen emergency expenses.

The goal of this exercise is to pay above anything that you pay as a renter. So on top of your normal housing bills, start to pay an additional amount based upon items like:

- Home mortgage
- Mortgage insurance
- Annual property taxes
- HOA (home owner association) fees
- Home furnishings

- Maintenance and repairs (even if you are moving into a new house, expect something to break down, because it will!)
- Cleaning
- Utilities

If you're currently renting, ask your landlord for all of the fees that he pays, and include those in your monthly budget. This budget is useful, too, when it actually comes time to make an offer on a home – you can present this budget to your lender for additional evidence that you can afford the loan since mortgage lenders like to see bank and credit card statements. Plus, it will give the bank confidence that you are a financially responsible adult that knows how to plan and budget.

Oh, and this is a great time to start collecting pay stubs and all financial statements in a folder that you will keep current as new information comes through the door.

4. Find a Lender AND GET PRE-APPROVED

Next to your real estate agent, the mortgage lender is the other most important professional you'll want to meet when it comes to buying a new home. A good real estate agent can introduce you to a good lender. I know several great ones!

How do you spot a good lender? Make sure you interview several candidates, check references, and **_don't allow anyone to run your credit score until you've picked a lender._** If several people try to access your score over a short period of time, your credit score can suffer.

By the way, avoid choosing a lender based on points. In fact, you might be tempted to work with an online lender because of low interest rates. DON'T. Online lenders – and their underwriters – are usually hard to contact and are not in control of the situation.

You'll just have to trust me on this one—I would much rather work with a lender that is a great communicator, is trustworthy, and is responsive to my needs than a lender who is none of those things, but offers a much lower interest rate.

If you're a first time homebuyer, the interest rate doesn't matter that much anyways—a difference of half a percent or even a full percent on a hundred thousand dollar home will make a small difference on your monthly payment. Do the calculation and use it to help you decide what a good lender is worth.

You're much better off choosing a lender based on quality of service and personality than you are by whoever is the cheapest.

Here's the most important thing: get pre-approved, *especially* if you are in a competitive seller's market (meaning there are less homes than there are buyers).

A good lender will help you understand all of your financing options, in addition to the pros and cons of each option.

This process will also help you align your budget (the one that you've been working on for the past four months, right?) and give you a practical idea of what you can and cannot afford.

A good lender is almost like a personal finance consultant. They won't just quote you the latest interest rate. They'll also guide you through the process to make sure you understand your options and make an informed decision on your mortgage. If your mortgage lender does *not* do this, find a new lender!

Once you've chosen a lender, sit down with them and have them walk you through your credit report.

5. Find a Real Estate Agent

A good real estate agent provides a number of services and brings a variety of benefits to you in your purchasing experience. Perhaps the most valuable of them all is *objectivity*. Think of the agent as that little angel sitting on your shoulder asking if that house with the infinity pool is really within your budget.

Of course, a good agent will guide you through the buying process. She can show you homes in neighborhoods that fit your requirements, and she should know the market and lead you to new listings before they even get on the market.

As you may already know, most home buyers start their search online. Eventually though, you are likely to end up working with an agent you know through a recommendation from family and friends.

It pays to *ask early* for recommendations and vet them early in the process. Even if you are six to nine months out from buying, finding a good agent can take some time, so the sooner you look, the better.

This means if you are planning on buying a home in September, you should be looking for an agent as early as January. Don't wait until the last minute.

Good agents can also help you bid if things become competitive, and bargain with the seller to get a fair price. This is especially true if they are requesting buyers without inspection or appraisal contingencies—*two things that will be the first to be dropped if you are in a competitive market.* That can be disconcerting figuring you may put an offer on a house that might not pass inspection or appraise for less than you are offering. In a seller's market, a good buyer's agent is crucial.

Other obstacles in the buying process are FHA financing (or other government programs) which take longer to close and can be prone to issues and delays.

Down-payment assistance programs, I'm looking at YOU.

Some sellers would prefer to accept a lower offer with a conventional mortgage than accept a higher offer with less certainty that the transaction will go through smoothly.

I've written extensively in this book about how to choose the *right* real estate agent. Make sure you read it cover to cover!

6. Be Ready

Once you've evaluated your credit score, worked on a new budget, contacted a real estate agent, and found a lender, it's time to start looking at houses.

<u>Unfortunately, most first time homebuyers do NONE of these things.</u>

They immediately go online and start looking for homes. Some even start driving around to check out properties they found online. This is a HUGE mistake, because you most likely have no idea what you qualify for, or what type of homes are suited to what types of financing.

Hopefully this chapter convinces you to take care of business *before* you actually start house hunting!

If you are shopping in a seller's market, you'll now understand why I recommend that you do everything above *first*. You must be ready to pounce on a great house when you find it. In hot markets, every day matters. Heck, sometimes every *hour* matters.

If you don't have your down payment, budget, and pre-approval, you might miss out on the perfect home.

And it's important during this time (it could take anywhere from three to six months) to keep your financial record *clean*. Don't make any major purchases, and keep on top of your bills. **The biggest mistake I've seen is buying a car within a year of buying a house.** Unless your income has gone up significantly since you financed your car, it will be very difficult to qualify for a mortgage if you already have monthly car payment obligations. So if you're driving a nicer, newer car, ask yourself if you'd rather have *that,* or own a home. Chances are you'd be better off driving a reliable used car, and putting the difference towards your dream of owning a home.

So, again, don't make any major purchases before applying for mortgage pre-approval. You don't want that final look at your finances to be disrupted.

<u>And before you actually make an offer on a house, do the following:</u>

- Call the utility providers (electric, water, sewer, garbage) to find out average monthly billing
- Find out about any potential homeowner association fees
- Look at the property taxes

Now, add all of those extra expenses to your budget, and ask yourself an honest question: **can you *still* afford the house?**

Here's the bottom line: don't fall for a beautiful home if the expenses are going to drive you over your budget. Don't let anyone push you to go into the upper ends of your budget, or over your budget. Even if you could technically afford the house, if you don't have any money left over, you are not going to be able to take care of the house.

Also avoid spending all your available cash on the down payment and closing costs. Otherwise, if you run into emergency repairs and unexpected costs, you will have to ask your family to bail you out, because the bank will not.

CHAPTER TEN

INVESTING IN RENTAL PROPERTY

ON THE NORTHSIDE

There is much to be said about buying investment property in general, and even more about buying it in a place like North Minneapolis. Let's start with some general and widely-applicable tips.

First of all, I highly recommend buying a property that is:

a) In good repair to begin with
b) On a block with high homeownership
c) Duplex is better than single-family, and triplex/fourplex are even better

Second of all, it is imperative for your long-term success that you run the numbers before you buy:

a) Calculate all expenses with as much specificity as possible
b) Budget in for reserves – make it a monthly expense and deduct it from your rental income (1-300 per unit per month)

c) Shop for financing options, if not starting with a home you have occupied

And third of all, if you are just starting out (or even if you are not) one of the best methods to ensure a solid investment is to begin with a home that you occupy or have occupied.

Buy a property that is in good repair:

I can't tell you how many clients I've had who've felt the lure of a fixer-upper. And I also have to admit that it's happened to me. Who can resist the pull of a beautiful true duplex, with matching floor plans that feature columned room-dividers, built-in buffets, and natural hardwood floors? So what if it has an octopus gravity heat unit, a bad roof, and needs new kitchens and baths, right? IT'S ONLY fifty thousand!

I have felt it. I have felt that lure. So I can relate. But here's the question to ask yourself: are you trying to get into the rental property business… or the restoration business?

Do you have a full time job?

Do you have children?

Do you have fifty thousand MORE dollars (in cash or form of a second loan) to put in two new kitchens, two new baths, a furnace and a roof?

Don't get in over your head. Buy a property that's in good repair. Painting and floor-sanding and landscaping are the types of things that might be fun (or at least not utterly painful) to add value and shine to your new rental property. Larger things might not be so much fun. And they surely will cost you a lot of time and money... BEFORE you can rent the building out and start seeing any income. So think long and hard about those sexy fixer-uppers.

Buy a property on a block with high homeownership:

Keep in mind that we are talking about North Minneapolis. Concentrations of rental are not a good idea. It might work in Uptown or North Loop or even Whittier, but North Minneapolis is predominantly made up of single-family homes, and those are not appropriate for clustering of rental.

Duplex is better than single-family – tri-plex or four-plex is better still:

The first property I ever bought was a duplex, and it was the best investment I ever made. I cannot overstate that fact. The rental income (which was very small back in those days) paid for my mortgage entirely, while I occupied one half. The subsequent appreciation (I sold it for five times what I paid) allowed me to expand into additional and larger properties in the years following my time there.

The thing about duplexes is that the maintenance and expenses are not much more than those for a single-family home, and yet you have two units, either to rent both or rent/occupy. It's a no-brainer.

The second property I ever bought was a four-plex. I was a little nervous, but I had heard another rental property owner whom I respected once say that he wished that the first building he ever bought had been a four-plex, rather than starting with single-family homes. His words stuck in my ears for four years, until I found one for myself.

And he was right.

Once again my husband and I lived in one unit while renting the other three. This time the income not only paid our mortgage, but also our expenses, with a tiny bit left over every month. And it was a beautiful building, which we took pride in maintaining and beautifying. After living there virtually for free for two years, we sold it for an eighty thousand dollar profit. (In hindsight it would have been a great property to keep and hold for many years. Alas, my husband and I were on the path to getting a divorce, so that was a driving factor in the sale.)

How to make your investment appreciate:

Many people will tell you that location is the most important consideration in buying rental property. Indeed, most will say that it should be the primary consideration for ANY real estate purchase. And they are right.

Since we're talking about the Northside, we've already broken rule number one by considering one of Minneapolis's least-desirable quadrants. However, you will find that people will still rank neighborhoods within the Near North and Camden communities for purposes of advising, warning or bragging about the best and worst for investing. In other words, even within the Northside, location matters, at least to most people. And it should to you too.

The truth is that if you are trying to attract quality renters to your property, and you want them to stick around, it will help to purchase a property on a block where they will feel safe. This might be in Victory, or it might be in Harrison, or it might be in Jordan. It really could be in any neighborhood, so long as the BLOCK on which it is located, and the roads your tenants take to get to and from home seem safe to them.

So the first step is to find that good-condition house, which is hopefully surrounded by at least a good number of invested homeowners, and then to do everything you can to help keep it clean, attractive and safe.

Too many investors treat North Minneapolis rental property as though it's a disposable sponge, ready to be wrung out repeatedly until it is so incapable of holding water that it must be thrown in the trash.

Don't be that investor.

For starters, it's not a good business practice. If you buy shoddy buildings for the purpose of squeezing your money and then some back out of it by renting to whomever comes along, allowing for crime to fester and your property to deteriorate further along the way, you WILL face issues. Residents of North Minneapolis have become increasingly intolerant of such exploitation of their communities and they have organized to stop it. Elected officials have taken notice, and slumlords are being targeted. Don't be that guy. It won't work anymore.

On the bright side, if you want to be a responsible property owner, maintaining and beautifying your building and carefully screening tenants with an eye toward keeping them around for the long-term, you will be welcomed and championed by other residents. And they will refer their quality renter friends and family to you, to boot.

One of the best ways to buy rental property is to start with a home that you occupy:

You've already seen that this is how I got started, by living in the properties that I purchased, and renting the other units. You've also seen that they appreciated greatly during the time that I owned them. But what you haven't seen is that there is a better strategy (presuming you are not divorcing your spouse) which is to buy, move in, move out, and HOLD.

For example, if after four years of living in my duplex, when I had decided that I wanted something different, I had attempted to buy that different something WITHOUT selling the duplex, I could have easily expanded my rental portfolio. And the reason this is a good way is that financing terms are better for owner-occupants. So, I got five percent down on my duplex when I bought it, because I was going to occupy it. If I had been buying it for investment, I would have had to put down twenty. And then after those four years, when I moved on to the four-plex, I again qualified for more favorable terms due to my desire to occupy it. See how that works?

Occupying first and then holding later is not the fastest way to amass a rental portfolio, but it may well be the safest and the best. It gives you time to get to know a property first-hand as you live in it, and furthermore, even those with the best of intentions for their rentals tend not to care for them as well as they care for their own homes. So make your investment property your own home – at least for a while. And make it beautiful. Those actions will pay you back in the form of better tenants, higher rents, and a nicer block. (To say nothing of happier and friendlier neighbors.)

Calculate all the expenses with as much specificity as possible:

There are rental worksheets galore on the internet, and I encourage everyone considering an investment property to use and compare them. But be sure to collect AS MUCH INFORMATION AS POSSIBLE, because the worksheets are only as good as the numbers you plug in. And even if you think you are not going to need a particular service (landscaping, for example) I suggest you include it anyway. You might have a tenant who loves to garden and keep the lawn up, but if that person doesn't stay forever, you will need to attend to the matter yourself or hire someone. Even at the most basic level, grass seed and gasoline for your lawnmower are not free. (And don't forget about the snow-blower, ice-melt, and shovels.)

Budget in for reserves:

Either the furnace will go out or your property will get ice dams or your tenants will cause some kind of damage. Or all of the above. Your garage might get graffiti-ed and the city might clean it up for you and send you a bill. Any number of things could happen. But one thing's for sure – you will pay for unanticipated issues. And sometimes that will be a lot. I have seen worksheets that suggest a fifty-dollar-per-month repair reserve. Don't be that naïve. Triple that number, at least. And consider the unique specificity of your units, and your building. You might want to budget more if they are large and/or have unique elements that could be more expensive to repair.

Shop for financing options

This point comes up again and again. It bears repeating. Shop around, shop around, shop around.

SECTION THREE

FOR SELLERS AND BUYERS

CHAPTER ELEVEN

WHO IS THE CLOSER AND WHAT IS THIS ABOUT TITLE INSURANCE?

By Lynn Gleason Oberpriller, Title-Smart

You've found the home you want, the purchase agreement has been signed, and your lender has ordered the appraisal.

Now what?

Once you have entered into a contract to purchase a home, part of the process will begin with the title and closing side of things. Most people assume it is smooth sailing until they own the house, but that is not always the case.

If you have a great closer and team who will watch all the details and trouble shoot any possible issues the process can be very pleasant (as it should be). However, if the correct documentation isn't received or if there are title issues, this can put a snag in to the process.

Most people don't have a clue what title insurance is. In simple terms, title is the formal documentation that shows proof of ownership to the property.

Title insurance is the protection against *prior title issue claims, including attorney fees* to clear up any title defects from the past.

Examples of some a title defects are: Old mortgages, heirs that have an interest in the property, liens from work that was completed (mechanics liens), judgments, state or federal tax liens, etc. Issues such as these can bring a closing process to a halt pretty quickly. Title insurance is basically protecting your interest in the property in the case of any problems that happened prior to your ownership.

To many consumers, title insurance seems like an added expense at closing. If you are getting a mortgage, the mortgage company will require you to get title insurance to insure the lender. As long as the title company did the research to be able to provide title insurance to the lender, they will offer you a policy as well, that protects <u>the portion of the home that is not covered by a loan, which is called your equity</u>.

This is called an owner's policy of title insurance, and it is optional.

If you spend the money for a one-time premium to cover any issues that arise with title later, you will not need to cover the costs of attorney's fees to clear it. The title company who issued the policy will clear it for you; that's why you bought the insurance!

When purchasing a bank owned property, purchasers believe that saving a few hundred dollars on an owner's policy is the way to go. The downside of saving that money is that many of the banks' title companies are closing the transactions in bulk and miss many details which can be caught but usually are not.

There can be a number of issues that come up during or after closing, when you are ready to sell.

An investor that I have closed for many times thought he'd save money on the owner's title insurance and for what he thought would ease the closing process. Little did he know, the title company did not record his deed or start any of the legal proceedings that are required to be done when a property goes through foreclosure. He is now trying to sell but can't because of the title company's lack of attention to detail and making sure that he was protected. <u>Saving a few hundred dollars is not worth the loss of potential buyers when you are ready to sell</u>. If you have a closer and title company that are skilled in finding any title defects, you will have the assurance that the ownership of the property is clear and you can purchase with piece of mind.

Another example of the biggest issues at closing are old mortgages still showing up on title. If the title company does a search of the records of the real estate and there are mortgages that are not showing satisfied and released, they have to be cleared before the closing can take place.

A seller I once closed for had six mortgages still showing on his title search when it was completed. The old mortgages were all from previous owners and at the time the loans were paid in full on property, the bank did not satisfy and release them (meaning, record a document at the county, called a satisfaction) in the real estate records.

An Owners Title Insurance policy protects a purchaser from previous owner's related title issues and any outstanding mortgages showing on title. If an Owners Title Insurance Policy was *not* purchased, each mortgage would need to be individually satisfied. This can take months to get taken care of…unless you have an Owners Title Insurance Policy.

Generally your title company is chosen by the Realtor in your purchase or sale. No matter if you are the seller or buyer, you can have your own closer. When selling, the closer and title company will clear any title issues on your behalf, order the accurate amounts to pay off your mortgages, and prepare all of your documents to transfer the title properly to the new buyer.

The difference when buying is that the closer is making sure that any title issues are resolved prior to your purchase, preparing all of the figures to make sure no liens can be filed on your property (unless you are obtaining a mortgage) and to determine the amount of money owing by the purchaser, and properly sign all of the loan documentation.

There are many small details that enter into the closing process and having a skilled closer is paramount.

When I am representing you for closing, I will be handling all the details with a smooth and stress free closing that I like to refer to as an "uneventful event" which is exactly how it should be.

CHAPTER 12

THE MORTGAGE CHAPTER

By Paul Basil, Megastar Financial

Back in the 1990s when I was first married and had a few bucks saved up, my wife thought it would be a good idea to get a house (she usually has the good ideas). I was thinking a boat would be cooler than a house.

She won.

I was not in the Real Estate industry at the time; I was a commodity trader. And, although I was a transactional expert, I knew little about the process of becoming a homeowner myself.

Like everyone else, I wanted to look at nice, pretty homes-- but was completely unable to determine whether or not I could even afford any home that appealed to us! Budget? What budget?!! I really had no idea what we could and couldn't afford.

An old friend of my wife's was our Realtor and he worked for a large real estate company in the Twin Cities. He connected us with a "Big Bank" lender that his firm had some kind of relationship with. We were on our way to getting answers!

Or so we thought.

We gave the Big Bank a check and a bunch of documents about our incomes as we continued to look at all kinds of homes in the areas we wanted to be in.

After a week, we had heard nothing and I had called a couple of times and pestered my Realtor too. I was told to wait. I become frustrated very quickly.

Fortunately, the father of my then business partner became aware of my plight. He recommended I call this fellow at a mortgage bank with whom he had had great luck. So I made the call.

What happened next was amazing…

On the call, he asked me some basic questions in order to get a credit report, and a few more about our down payment and income. I agreed to come by his office that afternoon with some documents. After I arrived he spent a few minutes explaining the mechanics and how a mortgage loan was very similar to an automobile loan.

Everything was EASY TO UNDERSTAND the way he explained it. During that transaction, I ended up learning a number of things. I learned that a mortgage loan was similar to a car loan in that the house/car is the collateral that secures the debt. I learned how mortgage rates are a by-product of the prices people are paying for bonds on Wall Street and that as bond prices rise, rates go down and vice-verse. I was instructed as to why I should not have made a major purchase just prior to house-hunting as the new account hurt my credit scores and also lowered the amount that we qualified for.

Talking to him was *nothing* like my experience with the "big bank." I actually left that meeting feeling empowered. I wasn't just a customer; I was a student. I had actually learned something!

I remember to this day sitting in his office answering a few more questions as he looked at my pay stubs. When he closed my file, he looked up at me, confirmed our price range, and said, "Go buy a house."

I said, "That's it?"

He nodded, smiled, pointed at the door, and simply said, "Go."

I was so glad that I had connected with this person who took an interest in me, my situation, and my level of understanding of the mechanics of the transaction. To this day, I see over and over that this kind of experience can only be found in a local, experienced Mortgage Banker.

So, years later when I made the decision to become a mortgage banker myself, it was my experience in buying that first home that gave me the vision of who I wanted to be (and who I did *not* want to be) as a mortgage banker.

My advice today? If you see a home purchase in your two-year time window, find a Mortgage Banker early in the process, especially if there are problems in your profile or your self-employment tax returns are complex. Find a Banker that you feel you can trust to meet your needs and get you answers you can count on. Your Mortgage Banker can help you set the stage for a future purchase by educating you and guiding you through the steps needed to ensure the best possible outcome when the time comes to move. Before you get too carried away in searching for a property, it is best to get pre-approved so you know what you are able to do. A pre-approval can take anywhere from five minutes to two years, depending on your profile and what you are trying to do. Again, it is never too early to check in with a good Mortgage Banker!

Your pre-approval will guide you to the next step; finding the home and writing the offer.

Once you are ready to make that purchase happen, income and asset documentation will be assembled with your credit report and dozen or so loan disclosures to form the base of the file that will be sent to an underwriter. The underwriter's job is to be sure that the loan meets or exceeds the requirements set forth in the loan guidelines (over a thousand pages). There are typically three phases after the decision is made to proceed with a transaction: Assembly (outlined above), review and conditions, and resubmission. The assembly of the underwriting file can be done in as little as one day if both you and your Banker are on their toes. (Typically though, clients take about a week to get their things in to us.) Next, the file is submitted to an underwriter. That underwriter will review your file and provide feedback as to what additional items she or he needs to approve your loan. This feedback is widely known as a 'conditional approval'. You and your lending team will work together to gather the required conditions and then resubmit for final approval. This entire process typically takes anywhere from five to fifteen business days.

Good luck and Happy Hunting!

CHAPTER THIRTEEN

HOW STAGING WILL GET YOU A <u>HIGHER PRICE</u> FOR YOUR HOME

Time and money.

Those are two things we can never have enough of, right?

And when we thinking about selling a house, pretty much all of us want to get the MOST amount of money in the LEAST amount of time, naturally.

So what if I told you that the homes which sell fastest are often also the ones selling for the MOST money?

(Wait – of course you already know that, since you read Chapter Four where we talked about the importance of pricing right for a speedy sale!)

But there is even more to it than that.

A Realtor who is knowledgeable about your particular market *and* knows how to look at the house with *buyers' eyes* to see exactly what should be done *before* listing can save you time, money, work and stress.

After writing the listing agreement, a competent Realtor will advertise your property, schedule showings with your approval, provide the necessary forms, represent you in negotiating a contract for purchase, show you what your expected net proceeds will be, keep you constantly informed of all activity on your property, and can arrange for closing services.

If time is an issue (as it should be, after all time is money), **getting a house ready for market is crucial.** Do not skimp on preparatory work in your rush to get the house up for sale, because you will pay for it in additional time on market. Make sure that EVERYTHING is ready to go in advance, so as to increase your chances of getting offers from the first buyers who walk through.

Those first buyers who come through your house are critical. They most likely have been shopping for a while, and may have already made an offer or two, and lost out. Mark my words – the most experienced buyers (and the ones most likely to write an offer after a single showing) are going to be some of the first people through your door. You don't want to still have painting and cleaning to do when they arrive. On the contrary, you want them to know immediately upon walking up to your front door that this is the home they've been waiting for!

Your Realtor *should* know how to make a house appeal to the senses. A lot of sellers need help in reaching that point. Don't feel bad about it – even some experienced Realtors need to bring outside eyes to their own homes when they are prepping to sell – the fact is that we get USED to our house, along with its little defects and perhaps the lack of styling in some rooms that we always meant to get to but never had the time for.

The other issue is that *some* Realtors are too timid to bring this issue up, for fear of offending clients and losing the listing.

<u>If your Realtor does not discuss the matter, make sure you ask them about it. Staging benefits you!</u>

The national average spent on staging a house is about one to three percent of the list price.

How well the house has been *maintained* is a huge factor, if the roof or basement leaks, those types of issues obviously are a higher priority than painting and redecorating.

It is important to remember that **staging is not covering up problems!**

Often, Realtors will provide the seller with a beginning list price and ask them to consider a price reduction if there are no offers within thirty days. This price reduction can be substantial **and unnecessary** if part of that money is spent up front on presenting the property at its best and making sure that the original price is on target rather than unrealistically bumped up to impress the sellers and secure the listing.

The National Association of Realtors states that those who generally spend one to three percent of the value of their home preparing their home to sell (staging), reap *eight to ten percent* in average price value, with fewer price reductions, carrying costs, or home sitting on the market. That is significant.

This formula shows that using *conservative* figures, if your home is worth two hundred fifty thousand and you spend one percent to stage it* ($2,500) ....you will then expect an eight percent return on your investment. Which is **twenty thousand dollars.**

Please understand that I am not making this up. If you are a sceptical seller, consider accompanying your agent on some listing previews. You will see what buyers' see – which is that the staged house is a) priced higher and b) sells faster.

This figure includes much more than staging fees, this includes new furniture, paying electricians, painters, and carpenters if needed.

Statistics show that staging your home for sale will shorten your market and bring you a higher price for your home. Period.

CONCLUSION

When I was a kid, growing up in the Kingfield neighborhood, my best friend lived a few blocks to the east. Her name was Ariel, and her house was conveniently located just on the other side of Martin Luther King Jr. Park. It worked out splendidly for playing together, because we could meet up at the park, or, later in our lives, at Curran's Restaurant just to the south, where we'd blow our couple of dollars in allowance on French fries and ice cream.

I remember getting a new bike, when I was about eleven years old. It was red, and shiny, and I was so ready to take it out exploring. The first stop I wanted to make was at Ariel's house. And after that, I was excited to see what was beyond. But my mother had some cautionary words first: She said *"you can ride your bike to the park, or to Curran's, or you can go west, toward Lake Harriet, or you can go south, toward the creek. But please do not go north, toward Lake Street, nor EAST, to Ariel's house."*

You see, even though my view of Ariel's house was that it was SO close, just on the other side of the park, my mother's view was that Ariel's house was ON THE OTHER SIDE OF INTERSTATE 35W. And so it was.

This was my first realization that Minneapolis had different neighborhoods, and that some were considered better than others. I didn't really know what was wrong with Ariel's neighborhood (Bryant) but I realized that my mother didn't think it was safe for me to ride my bike over there.

I don't tell this story to pick on my mother. God bless her, she has watched me purchase homes and live in all the most challenged neighborhoods in this city, starting with Phillips in South Minneapolis and working my way over into and through several North Minneapolis neighborhoods. She has seen that not all of these neighborhoods even come close to the stereotypes we once wrote off as truth, from the relatively sheltered southwest corner of our city.

The reason I tell this story is to underscore the fact that we all rely on generalizations to one degree or another, for simplicity's sake. Whether it is about which neighborhoods are "good" or what kind of people shop at Wal-Mart versus Byerly's, or what sort of a job a person has by the vehicle they drive.

But if we are interested in something, and open to learning more, we can often find many delightful exceptions to such over-simplistic generalizations. I have found this to be true in North Minneapolis.

This book is ultimately about buying and selling homes. As we have seen, the vast majority of my advice can be applied to any neighborhood... and even to the suburbs. There are many core principles of real estate sales that do not change, regardless of where the property is located.

I hope that these principles have been helpful and clearly-stated, and that you have learned some things about the way the process works, as well as how to maximize your potential in a real estate transaction, whether you are a buyer or a seller.

I also hope that since you are reading this book, you are interested in challenging the stereotypes about North Minneapolis. Whether you end up on James Avenue North, Wentworth Avenue

South, Tyrol Hills or Historic Stillwater, it is enough for me that you know how richly diverse our neighborhoods, housing stock and community are. And that you help spread the word.

ACKNOWLEDGEMENTS

The first few properties I ever showed in North Minneapolis were bank-owned, and listed by agents who clearly weren't interested in doing their best. The homes were listed very cheaply, which is likely one of the reasons for the lackluster care they received. Several had been broken into, and one actually had squatters actively inhabiting it. I remember thinking is this how things are done over here?

Thankfully, I soon learned that that was not in fact how things are always done. There are several great agents working on the Northside, for whom the addresses on their listings constitute a basis for pride, not embarrassment. I have had the great pleasure to work with many of them, and am always delighted when those opportunities arise.

In particular, Deb Wagner, Sandy Loescher, Jean & Tom Bain, and Stephanie Gruver come to mind. All of these agents not only work in North Minneapolis, but in fact also live here. The integrity and professionalism that these agents possess both inspire and motivate me on a regular basis. And they are not the only ones.

So, if you are looking to buy or sell on the Northside and you find that the Realtors with whom you consult are not exhibiting the enthusiasm you expect, consider working with a Northside agent. There are several of us here.

I must also acknowledge my broker, Steve Havig, whose infectious positivity and enthusiasm for the urban environment have made Lakes Area Realty the best company for which I have ever worked. Everything is more fun when Steve is around. Were it not for him, this book would never have been written. And *that*, as my husband would say, *is the truth, Ruth*.

CONTACT US:

Constance Vork, Associate Broker

Lakes Area Realty of Minneapolis

612-396-4046 mobile

constance@lakesarearealty.com

Lynn Gleason Oberpriller, Executive Closer

Title-Smart, Inc.

612-940-0978 direct

lynn@title-smart.com

Paul Basil, Loan Officer

NMLS 452480

Megastar Financial Corporation

763-999-7999 office

pbasil@megastarfinancial.com

Made in the USA
Charleston, SC
12 July 2014